C0-DVT-209

THE NEW HOUSE

BUYER'S GUIDE

© 1986 William Marchiony

All Rights Reserved

No part of this book may be reproduced in any form, or by any means, without written permission from the publisher.

II

Published by Carefree Living Co.
2509 East Thousand Oaks Blvd., #160
Thousand Oaks, CA 91362-3249.

Printed in the United States of America by
State Printing & Publishing, Inc.
Westlake Village, CA 91362-3918.

Cover design by Ginger Osgood Worthley, MFA

Library of Congress Catalog Card Number: 86-70558

ISBN number: 0-938411-00-4

$18.95

To my wife and best friend Anne, without whose loving support, professional help and constant encouragement this book might never have gone beyond just being an idea.

III

THE NEW HOUSE BUYER'S GUIDE

WILLIAM MARCHIONY

CONTENTS

ACKNOWLEDGMENTS

COVER DESIGN: Special thanks to Ginger Osgood Worthley, MFA, who brought her 30 years as a professional printmaker, painter and sculptor to this endeavor. Beyond that, I am grateful for her many hours of editorial help and for our long-standing friendship.

COVER, HOUSE RENDERINGS: Courtesy of Best-Selling Home Plans, HOME MAGAZINE, Knapp Communications Corp., 5900 Wilshire Blvd, Los Angeles, CA 90036-5013, with sincere appreciation to Ann Hope, Publishing Director, for her extensive research and cooperation.

PRINTING: Howard K. Smith, President, State Printing and Publishing, Inc. 31300 Via Colinas, Westlake Village, CA 91362-3918, has been much more than a printer. Howard has led me patiently and helpfully through the maze of unforeseen obstacles in the world of printing and publishing. With his guidance and expertise, this effort has been a pleasant and enjoyable experience.

GLOSSARY: Taken in part from: CONSTRUCTION DICTIONARY, published and distributed by the Greater Phoenix, AZ Chapter of the National Association of Women in Construction (NAWIC). 6th edition, 2nd printing (1986) available from the organization at P.O. Box 6142, Phoenix, AZ 85005-6142, $21.00 prepaid, including postage and handling.

INSURANCE INFORMATION: Generously provided by John M. DeNegre, National Appraisal Manager, Personal Insurance Division, Chubb Group of Insurance Companies, P.O. Box 1615, Warren, NJ 07061-1615.

General Contractor's Licensing regulations information compiled with the help of SUMMARY of STATE REGULATIONS and TAXES affecting GENERAL CONTRACTORS, published by American Insurance Association, 85 John Street, New York, NY 10038-2879, and National Association of State Contractors Licensing Agencies, P.O. Box 14088, Baton Rouge, LA 70898-4088.

INTRODUCTION

The waiting is almost over! You have watched your new house or condominium being built and now that it is nearing completion, you will soon be scheduling your detailed inspection of the house before accepting it from the builder.

As a NEW HOUSE BUYER, no matter where you live in the United States, this book is especially designed and written for you. If you have already taken title to your new home, the book will still be very useful to you in pointing out defects that perhaps you missed during your final examination. (See MESSAGE TO A NEW HOMEOWNER at the end of this section)

This step-by-step book was expressly written to assist you BEFORE and AS you take a most important WALK that leads to being a happy homeowner.

As a NEW HOUSE BUYER, you should be well prepared for this walk: when your dream home has been finished, but before the legal settlement has been completed and the title transferred to you, you will be asked to take a tour, or a "walk-through", of your new house with your builder's representative. This person might be the job superintendent, the customer service manager or whomever the builder designates.

The importance of this "walk-through" cannot be overemphasized. It is your best, and perhaps last, opportunity to examine the house in minute detail and point out defects in materials or workmanship to the builder's representative.

At this point, you still have a considerable amount of financial "clout" on your side to get these things corrected: the builder wants his money and, before he gets it, you need to accept the house.

Part I is a textbook. This should be read in ADVANCE of your final meeting with the builder as there are many tips, pointers and suggestions to help you avoid the usual pitfalls and make it a pleasurable experience.

Part II is a workbook. It has been designed to be used in practice sessions and finally "in the field" during your scheduled walk-through. You should take the time to practice because your actual walk-through could be your LAST OPPORTUNITY to list defects that need correcting. Before going on practice sessions, make photocopies of the walk-through sheets so that you will have the originals for the real walk-through.

Reading the text of this book will give you the overall picture of what to look for in each and every room and area before you sign your acceptance of the house from the builder. By following the instructions and suggestions given here, you will be able to recognize the most common problems that could arise.

Schedule your walk-through during daylight hours and DO NOT allow yourself to be rushed through this important inspection. Plan on spending an hour and a half, or more if you need it, to examine everything in detail.

When you go on your walk-through, leave the kids at home or with a baby sitter. This is a time when you need to concentrate on the task at hand and you can't do the job properly with any distractions. Don't take friends or relatives along, either.

XII

You (the owner/s) and the builder's representative should be the only ones there. Of course, if you have hired an inspector to help you, he or she should also accompany you. The tagging along of others, just to be sociable, or to add their opinions, can be very time-consuming and counter-productive.

If you are buying in a development, look carefully and study the model so you get a clear picture in your mind of how your house should look. When going through the model, don't allow yourself to be side-tracked by the decorator items and accessories which you may not have ordered.

We have all heard the "horror" stories from friends and relatives about their experiences with the purchase and subsequent occupancy of their newly constructed house. There may be some builders who instruct their representatives to write down for correction only those items which the buyer finds during the tour through the house and not to point out any defects.

Today, however, this practice is less frequent since most reputable builders are becoming more and more consumer oriented. In this era of "consumerism", builders are stressing the importance of the walk-through, and voluntarily pointing out defects that perhaps the buyer might not have noticed. Their philosophy is that "word of mouth" advertising, through a satisfied buyer, is their best form of advertising.

Most building contractors and tract developers do a very acceptable job on 95% of the house. It is in the completion of the myriads of details which comprise the last 5% when many of them run into problems in the scheduling and intensive supervision necessary to complete the job as it should be done.

Many states now have set up licensing requirements for General Contractors. The licensing effectiveness, so far as the consumer is concerned, varies from state to state. Some states require a license only for the purpose of providing additional revenue. Other states give examinations to the prospective licensees and then monitor their performance after licensing.

It is interesting to note that, in contrast to the sporadic requirements for licensing of General Contractors, **ALL 50** states have set up Consumer Protection Agencies. In the absence of state licensing laws, the consumer can contact this agency for help with their particular problem.

Chapter 12 contains the name and address of each state's Consumer Protection Agency, as well as the states which require the licensing of General Contractors. We sincerely hope that the information you learn from this book will enable you to recognize the problems in your new house so well that you will not need to resort to your state agencies for assistance.

These listings are based upon information available at the time of publication, and no guarantee as to the accuracy or completeness is given or implied. We commend and congratulate any state that has added agencies or added additional requirements for the regulation of General Contractors, either during or subsequent to this publication.

XIII

MESSAGE TO A NEW HOMEOWNER

While reading this book, as a NEW OWNER, you may have discovered things that you **should have seen** during your walk-through.

Any problem areas that you find now may still be corrected by your builder. Most builders offer at least a one year warranty on the house. If you are still within your warranty period, contact your builder and ask that the items you found be corrected.

Since you have already moved into your new house, you should be fair with your builder and limit your requests for repairs to items not damaged by you during your occupancy!

ABOUT THE AUTHOR

Over 25 years in residential real estate brokerage, combined with supervisory positions in the construction industry, have gone into the writing of this book. My special construction expertise, in the area of "final finish", focused on the last 5% of the building job as Finish Superintendent, Quality Control Manager, Customer Service Manager or Field Superintendent.

I personally have seen the best and the worst workers at their appointed tasks. I know most of the "tricks" used to disguise shoddy workmanship and I don't want you, the reader, to suffer from the mistakes of incompetent tradespersons. It is now time to share this expertise with those buyers who are not knowledgeable in this field.

PART I

ALL ABOUT THE WALK-THROUGH

Most builders or contractors will have their own walk-through sheet on which they list the items that need correction. Toward the back of this book, you will find work sheets that you can use while conducting your walk-through. They are most comprehensive in that they may list many areas or items to inspect that possibly might not be incorporated in your house. Use these sheets anyway and just cross out the items that are not applicable and add anything that is not listed.

Be certain that the builder's representative writes down on his or her checklist, or walk-through form, all of the items that need correcting or replacing so that there is a WRITTEN record of everything.

When the walk-through is completed, compare your work sheets with the builder's to make sure that his contain the same items as yours. When both you and the builder's rep sign his walk-through sheets, make sure you get a legible copy. This becomes especially important after you have moved in and you call the builder's customer service department with a problem.

If any condition was not spelled out during the walk-through, they may take the position that it is something that you caused during or after you moved in. Then they will classify it as a "maintenance item" for which they would not be responsible.

This particularly applies to nicks and scratches in the paint, scrapes or dents in the walls or ceilings, gouges or tears in the the floor covering, cracked ceramic tiles, chipped or dented appliances, cracked or broken window glass, missing screens, etc. It is readily understandable that these dings and damages could and may have been done during your move-in either by you accidentally or by your mover. The builder wants to protect himself from having to repair something that was not his fault.

Items that would not fall into this category, and which would still remain the builder's responsibility are plumbing leaks, electrical problems, heating or cooling malfunctions, or any other problem which may develop that obviously could not have been caused by your occupancy of the house.

Appliances, ie. ovens, range, microwave oven, barbeque, broiler, trash compactor, dishwasher, refrigerator, washer, dryer, garbage disposal, garage door opener, ceiling fans, heating and air conditioning equipment, etc, are covered by each manufacturer's warranty. These warranties will usually be serviced (honored) by the particular sub-contractor who installed them. Operating instructions and owner's manuals on all of your appliances should be given to you at this time.

Ask your builder for a list of the service companies who will perform any necessary warranty service on these items. Also, if you haven't already been told, have the builder's representative show you the locations of the circuit breaker panel, gas meter, water meter and the main water shut-off valve.

2

At the conclusion of the walk-through, you will be asked to sign the walk-through inspection sheet. This form will essentially state that you are accepting the house from the builder, as is, subject to the defects listed thereon being corrected, repaired or replaced by the builder within a reasonable period of time.

Be sure to compare the builder's walk-through sheet with yours to make certain that nothing was overlooked.

It is reasonable to expect that most of the items on the list will be corrected in about 30 days from the date of your walk-through. Unless you are moving in immediately, the builder will, most likely, be anxious to get as many items corrected while the house is unoccupied. It is easier for him and his sub-contractors to work on the house when no one is living there.

You should not, however, be unduly concerned if it takes 30 days or even longer. Keep in mind that your house was built and assembled by many sub-contractors and tradespeople and it sometimes takes the builder longer to schedule them back for repairs than it did to do the original work.

After the walk-through is completed, and you have signed the acceptance, you can make your plans to move in after the final title settlement. If the utilities (gas, electric, water) are not turned on, find out from the builder's representative if the final inspection has been made by the local building inspector, and if the house has been approved for occupancy.

If you are told that the house has been approved for occupancy, it might be wise for you to call the gas and electric companies to have them check their records to see that they have been notified by the inspector's office. If they have no record of the approval, tell your builder and he will contact the inspector to have the matter resolved.

At this time, schedule a turn-on date with the utility companies so that when you are ready to move in, there will be service. It usually takes them a few days to accomplish the turn-on, so it is wise to plan ahead.

Do this before you plan to occupy the house because the service on your utilities will not begin until the building inspector has given both the gas and electric companies his final approval.

BASIC FUNCTION OF THE BUILDING INSPECTOR

In most areas of the country the progress of construction during its many stages is monitored by inspectors employed by the municipality, city or county in which the construction is being done. It is the inspector's duty to see that the work being performed is in accordance with the building codes and regulations that pertain to that particular jurisdiction.

In large city and county areas, the various stages of construction may be handled by many different inspectors who are specialists in that particular trade. These individual inspections will probably include initial and final property grading, foundation and retaining wall footings, framing, insulation, plumbing, electrical and mechanical (heating, ventilating & air conditioning).

The "main" inspector is the one whose responsibility it is to see that the inspection sheet or card is signed by the other inspectors upon satisfactory completion of the work performed in their area of jurisdiction. After the building is completed, the main inspector will make his final inspection and approve the building for occupancy.

KEEP IN MIND THAT THE BUILDING INSPECTOR IS NOT CONCERNED WITH "COSMETIC" APPEARANCES. THE INSPECTOR IS ONLY CHECKING ON ITEMS THAT RELATE TO THE CONFORMANCE TO CODES AND THE BUILDING SAFETY.

In smaller jurisdictional areas, all of these inspection functions may be handled by one person who is knowledgeable in all of the trades involved. In some states, when you are outside the city limits of the large urban areas, there may not be ANY building codes and regulations. In that event, there will be no protective inspections made during the course of construction and you will have to rely upon the integrity of your builder.

You should investigate to find out if residential construction in the area you have chosen is regulated by any governmental agency and, if so, which one and where it is located. You may never have a reason to contact them directly, but you should know in case personal contact becomes necessary.

If your investigation reveals that your area is not covered by any building codes or inspections, you should consider protecting yourself in the following manner:

1. Check out the reputation of your builder or contractor by visiting people who have purchased homes from that company, as any reputable builder should be cooperative in supplying you with names and addresses.

2. If there is a BETTER BUSINESS BUREAU in the area, talk to them to see if any complaints have been filed with them against the builder and the nature of the complaint(s).

3. If your state licenses residential building contractors, follow the same procedure as in 2. above with the State Contractors Licensing Agency.

4. As a further protection, you may find it advisable to hire an independent inspector to examine the construction either upon final completion or during the various stages. The fee you pay him or her will be money wisely spent.

Most local telephone directories will have a listing called "Building Inspection Service." Ask your lending institution, bank, savings and loan or mortgage company for a list of names. Be sure you are specific: you want names of Independent Building Inspectors, **not** Appraisers.

The chapters that follow will cover specific items that you should examine in detail in each area of the house and grounds.

4

THE KITCHEN

This room is the one that most likely will require very careful examination. As the nerve center of the house, it contains more items to be examined and more possibilities for error than any other area of the house. There are more building trades involved here than in any other room, and the greater number of people who are working here, the more chances there are for mistakes and omissions to be made.

KITCHEN FLOORS

Let's start with the floor. There are five types of floor coverings that are most commonly used: 1. Ceramic tile; 2. Vinyl or vinyl asbestos tile or asphalt tile; 3. Vinyl sheet goods (one piece). 4. Wood; 5. Carpet.

CHECK POINTS FOR ALL: First, regardless of which of these types of material you have chosen, be sure that the pattern and color are what you have selected. Carefully check to see that there are no scratches, gouges or cracks. The areas to concentrate on are in front of the appliances-range, oven, dishwasher, compactor, etc. The reason for this is that the floor covering is most always installed BEFORE the appliances and some of the workmen may not have been too careful when the appliances were slid into place. These units are heavy and if not handled properly, can damage the floor.

CERAMIC TILE

CHECK POINTS:

1. If your floor is ceramic tile, the first things to look for are cracked or chipped tiles. Chipping is most likely to occur where the tiles end; that is where the tile meets some other type of flooring, such as carpet.

2. If there is a step down or a step up from the kitchen to another room, inspect these edges carefully as they are vulnerable to chipping.

3. Cracks in the tile can occur in any area and are usually caused by a heavy object having been dropped onto the surface.

4. Look at the grout joints. These are separation spaces between the tiles and the grout is the cement-like material that fills these spaces. Are the joints even and symmetrical? Is all of the grout the same color throughout?

5. Are all of the tiles the same height? When one or more tiles are higher than the rest, this will lead to early chipping of the edges of these particular tiles and it is also uncomfortable to walk on them.

VINYL TILE, VINYL ASBESTOS TILE, ASPHALT TILE

CHECK POINTS:

6

1. See that the pattern is laid down symmetrically. Does it match and does the pattern follow its intended design?

2. See that all of the tile edges run in a straight line and that each square matches the one next to it. Do all the tiles look like they are the same color? If the shading varies, the installer may have used boxes from different factory runs. Write it down on your list and have the builder contact his floor covering contractor to correct the problem.

3. Are any of the corners lifting up? This may not be a problem, even though it may not look right to you. If the covering was installed during cold weather and is on a concrete slab, these edges will usually flatten out a few days after the heat is turned on in the house. You might also experience a "crackling" sound when you walk across the tile floor. This also will usually disappear when the house has been warmed for a few days.

4. Make sure that the molding called "base shoe" has been installed. This is a molding that is attached to the baseboard molding and its purpose is to hide the gaps left where the flooring material meets the wall. This base shoe molding gives a finished look to the flooring installation.

VINYL SHEET GOODS

If vinyl sheet goods was your choice, the chances are that the area is large enough to make it necessary to require two or more pieces to cover the entire floor.

CHECK POINTS:

1. Make sure that the seams are hardly visible.

2. Be certain that the seams are securely cemented with no loose edges.

3. Check to see that the pattern matches and that all of the material runs in the same direction.

4. As in item 4 above, see that the base shoe molding has been installed.

WOOD

If you have wood floors, you have chosen a very durable floor covering. With proper care, it will last many years. If you are in the habit of walking around the kitchen in your bare or stocking feet, you will find that a wood floor feels much warmer to the touch than vinyl or ceramic tile.

Modern wood kitchen floors are usually installed by glueing the finished flooring to the sub-floor with a special bonding material. Many patterns and designs are available. They range from long strips laid side-by-side to square sections laid in a pattern arrangement, known as parquet.

7

CHECK POINTS:

1. Make sure that the pattern used is symmetrical.

2. Look for any gouges or deep scratches, especially in front of the appliances. This area is most vulnerable to damage.

3. Whether your floor was pre-finished at the factory or stained and lacquered on the job, check the finish to see that it is evenly applied.

4. Look to see that the base shoe molding has been installed, and that it is stained and finished to match the flooring.

CARPET

Carpet in the kitchen can be a very attractive and practical selection for the floor covering. The fabrics that have been developed are resistant to most any type of stain and they are also extremely durable.

CHECK POINTS:

1. Make sure that the pattern that is installed was the one that you selected.

2. Look for seams in the carpet. They should be almost invisible.

3. Since this type of carpet is glued down, check to see that there are no bulges or loose areas.

4. See that the base shoe molding has been installed where the carpet meets the wall.

5. Look for any imperfections in the pattern design or in the fabric itself.

CEILING & LIGHTING

Most kitchen lighting installed today is in the form of florescent fixtures that transmit their light through translucent plastic panels installed in suspended wood or metal frames.

CHECK POINTS:

1. Look for broken or cracked panels.

2. Examine the frame that holds the panels, making sure that the frame fits tight against the ceiling and that it is not scratched, dented, bent or gouged.

3. Check the rest of the ceiling that is not taken up with the lighting panels. Make sure it is smooth and symmetrical and that no joints are visible.

KITCHEN COUNTER TOPS

The counter tops will either be ceramic tile, laminated plastic(formica) or a combination of both.

CHECK POINTS:

1. See that none of the tiles are chipped or cracked.

2. Pay particular attention to the edges around the sink and the front edges of the counter. This is where damage is most likely to occur.

3. Look to see that all of the tiles are the same height and that there are no sharp edges.

4. If your counter top is laminated plastic (Formica) look for chipped edges or scratches.

5. Check to make sure that none of the edges are loose.

KITCHEN APPLIANCES

Let us now proceed to a close examination of the appliances. Even though the sink is really not an appliance, let's include it here.

CHECK POINTS:

1. Inspect the sink for chips, scratches and dents in the porcelain finish or stainless steel surface.

2. Look all around the edges and particularly on the inside front where it is hard to see unless you look carefully.

3. Examine the dishwasher's front panels for scratches and dents.

4. Look at the inside for the same things and make sure that all of the dish racks are there and that they operate smoothly. Look at the top edge of the front panel. This trim panel will sometimes get scratched if the installation is not done correctly.

5. Make sure that the dishwasher is fastened securely in the cabinet opening. You can check this by trying to move it from side to side. Now stand back as far as you can and visually examine it to see that it is level with the floor and the counter top.

6. Next, check the range and oven(s). Again, examine all of the panels for scratches and dents and check the inside to see that all of the racks are there. Whether you have a single range, double eye-level or counter top range and built-in oven, check them all to see that they are installed securely and that they are level. If the oven doors have glass panels, make sure that the glass is not cracked. Whether your range is gas or electric, see if all the parts are there - control knobs, burner, grates, etc.

7. If you have a hood over the range or oven, check to see that this unit is securely fastened to the cabinet. In the case of an eye-level double oven and range combination, the hood will probably be fastened to the top of the range. Look in the cabinet above the hood and make sure that the hood is vented to the outside. It is vented if you see a pipe going from the top of the hood inside the cabinet up through the ceiling or out the back wall of the hood cabinet. This step is, of course, if the unit is designed for outside venting. Some hoods are self-venting and do not require this connection. An examination of the owner's manual will tell you whether or not it is a self-venting type.

8. Be sure to check carefully any other appliances that you may have in the kitchen such as a refrigerator, trash compactor, barbeque broiler, microwave oven, etc. Make sure all the parts are there and there are no scratches or dents.

9. Last, but certainly not least, you want to look over the cabinets very carefully. First, check for scratches, gouges, and missing door and drawer pulls. Many cabinets are delivered prefinished from the cabinet manufacturer and they are installed early in the completion of the kitchen. This leaves them

9

vulnerable to all kinds of careless damage. Minor scratches can usually be touched up by the builder's customer service people, but if they are badly scratched, insist on replacement panels, drawer fronts or doors.

10. Next, examine each door of the cabinets to see that it opens and closes properly and that it is not warped. If the top closes tight against the frame and the bottom sticks out and does not meet flush with the frame, it is a pretty good bet that the door is warped and should be replaced. Very minor warping can be corrected by a hinge adjustment. *Leave this to the cabinet experts and do not attempt to correct warpage yourself.* Open and close all the drawers and make sure they all operate smoothly. See that when the drawers are closed that the fronts line up even with the cabinet frame.

11. Open the cabinet under the sink and look for water spots or leaks and also check to see that the basket strainers and faucet aerators are installed.

3

BATHROOMS POWDER ROOM LAUNDRY ROOM

There are many things to look at in the bathrooms, powder room, and laundry room. The following items should be examined carefully:

SINKS AND TUBS

CHECK POINTS:

1. Look for any cracks or chips in the surface or edges of the sinks or tubs.Turn the faucets on and off. Do they operate easily and smoothly? Be sure they do not drip.

2. Does the drain stopper work and will it hold water in the sink or tub when closed. (CLOSE THE STOPPER AND PARTIALLY FILL THE TUB AND SINK TO BE SURE THEY BOTH HOLD WATER.)

3. If the hot water is on in the house, make sure that HOT water comes out of the spout when the **left** faucet is opened. (Sometimes plumbers make mistakes when they install the rough plumbing, and will inadvertently reverse the pipes). This problem should be corrected by the plumber.

4. While you are checking hot and cold water, you might also make sure that the toilet tank is fed with cold water. This type of mistake, where hot water is fed into the tank, is rare, but it does happen.

Note: I should point out here that in extremely cold climates where temperatures are consistently sub zero for long periods of time (Alaska and many Northern states) the toilet tank water is a blend of hot and cold water which is mixed together through a special valve. The reason for this is that if very cold water is fed to the tank when the inside house temperature is 70 degrees or more, any moisture in the warm air will condense on the cold tank and drip onto the floor.

COUNTER TOPS

CHECK POINTS:

1. The counter tops may be one of the several commonly used materials: ceramic tile, laminated plastic (such as Formica) or a type of imitation marble. In all cases look carefully at the edges for chips. In the case of ceramic tile, inspect for cracked tiles and also see that the grout has been applied evenly. If the counters are laminated plastic or cultured marble (artificial), be particularly careful to look for scratches in the surface. Some workmen are not careful and may have stood on the counter for one reason or another, without a protective covering under their shoes.

LIGHTING

CHECK POINTS:

1. Luminous light panels installed in the ceiling are used in most bathroom lighting. These are florescent lights under which are placed translucent plastic panels, mounted in either metal or wood frames. This type of fixture gives adequate lighting with minimum glare. If your room has this type of lighting, look to see that there are no chips or cracks in the plastic panels and that the frames are not bent or broken.

2. If the standard type of ceiling or wall mounted fixtures have been installed, make sure that all of the parts are installed and that no glass shades or panels are missing or broken.

TRIM

CHECK POINTS:

1. Have the shower heads, faucet aerators, toilet seats, paper holders and towel bars been installed? Some builders install these items just prior to move-in time and they are contained in what is called a "move-in kit."

   The kit will usually also contain the kitchen sink basket strainers, garbage disposal stopper, fireplace gas valve key and other miscellaneous items that may become lost or stolen if they are installed before move-in time.

2. **Toilet**
   a. Examine the top of each toilet seat lid for scratches and gouges. The top of the lid is a very convenient place for a careless worker to stand when there is no ladder or stool nearby. If you find any scratches or gouges, ask that the seat be replaced.

   b. Lift the seat up and down to see that it operates smoothly. Look at the bottom of the seat to make sure that the seat bumpers are there. The seat bumper is a rubber or plastic spacer that keeps the seat from resting directly on the rim of the bowl.

12

c. Flush the toilet to make sure that the waste lines are clear of any stoppages.

3. **Medicine Cabinet**
   a. Carefully inspect the medicine cabinet. It may be made of painted metal, chrome plated, wood framed door, single or double door style. Look at the mirrors carefully for cracks, chips or any imperfections in the glass.

   b. Next examine the frame to see that it is not cracked or dented. Open and close the cabinet door to make sure that it operates smoothly and see that the latch works properly. Look to see that all the shelves are installed. In a standard sized cabinet, you would normally find three shelves. Probably the cabinet will be of the recessed variety. This means that the main cabinet portion is set into the wall. Look at this area carefully to make sure that the frame fits tightly against the wall and that there are no spaces between the frame and wall.

WALLS

CHECK POINTS:

1. If your bathroom and/or shower walls are ceramic tile, look for broken or cracked tiles; also check the grout between tiles to see, that it is uniformly applied. Look carefully around the light switches and the electrical outlets to make sure that there are no spaces between the tile and the switch or outlet cover. If there are spaces, note this on your list as this defect should be corrected.

13

FLOOR COVERING

CHECK POINTS:

1. **Ceramic tile:** look for chips or cracks in the tile and and see that the grout has been neatly and evenly applied.

2. **Carpeting:** does it look as though it has been neatly installed? Does it fit properly around the toilet bowl?

3. **Vinyl:** look to see that the pattern appears uniform and that there are no scratches or gouges. Make sure that the base shoe molding has been installed around the edges where the floor meets the wall.

LAUNDRY ROOM

CHECK POINTS:

1. Just as you did in the bathrooms, check the laundry room walls and ceilings for uniformity and good appearance. In addition, look to see that there is adequate lighting.

2. Examine the area where the washer and dryer will be installed. In this space, you should find a 110 volt electrical outlet for your appliances; hot and cold water faucets and a drain pipe for the waste water from your washing machine; and, for your clothes dryer, an exhaust vent, and either a gas connection or a 220 volt outlet.

3. Check whether your house will have a gas or an electric dryer connection. Then make sure that your dryer uses the same energy source which is supplied. For example, if the dryer you presently own is gas, and there is only a hook-up for an electric dryer, you will need to dispose of the gas dryer and buy an electric one.

4

CEILINGS AND WALLS

The two types of ceiling and wall surfaces we will discuss here are those which are most commonly used:

DRYWALL
LATH AND PLASTER.

Prior to the invention and development of drywall (also called plasterboard or sheetrock) most wall and ceiling surfaces were made by the application of plaster.

PLASTER, easily defined, is a mixture of sand, water, gypsum plaster and hydrated lime. This mixture is applied in a wet, plastic state and it dries to a smooth, solid surface. During the final coating process, it can be textured to produce varied surface patterns.

LATH merely refers to the surface over which the plaster is applied. Originally, the application of lath consisted of wood strips nailed to the vertical studs or ceiling joists with spaces in between each slat. The first or "scratch" coat is squeezed between the slats and when it becomes hard, a mechanical bond is created between the plaster and the backing. The use of lath and plaster is a more expensive and time-consuming job than the installation of drywall.

DRYWALL is manufactured by bonding sheets of paper to the front and back of a layer of plaster. This drywall board comes in standard sized sheets four feet in width and either eight, twelve or fifteen feet in length and in various thicknesses. The name drywall came into usage for the obvious reason that it is attached to the studs or beams in a "dry" state as opposed to the original wet plaster application.

Most houses, commercial and industrial buildings are built with drywall today. It is quicker to install, more economical and easier to repair. It also withstands considerably more movement before cracking than will plaster.

There are many pros and cons concerning plaster versus drywall and vice versa, but we won't go into these here because you probably will not have a choice anyway. If your home is being built in a development or tract, the builder will have already made the decision and the chances are more than likely that it will be drywall. We will, therefore, limit our discussion here to drywall construction except to say that if your walls are plaster, the things to look for are smoothness of the surfaces. If they are textured, see that the design looks uniform. Also, check to make sure there are no cracks in the surface.

CEILINGS

Chances are that the ceiling's surface finish on your house will probably be what is called "blown accoustic" and, in construction slang sometimes called "cottage cheese" or "popcorn" since it does somewhat resemble those items.

Look to see that the entire surface of the ceiling is uniform. There should not be any thick or thin areas. This means there should not be any thick "lumps" or areas so thin that the area is not covered uniformly. There should not be any scratches or gouges in the surface.

16

This accoustic material is applied to the ceiling fairly early in the finish process because it is a messy operation. Because of the early installation, the ceilings are prone to careless damage, such as someone scraping the surface while carrying a door, or other long piece of equipment, into the room.

Look to see that the area where the ceiling meets the side walls is neat and clean. There should be a definite line of demarcation and no accoustic material should extend down onto the wall surface.

In the kitchen, bathrooms, powder room and laundry area, the ceilings will, no doubt, be smooth and painted with enamel paint. The reason that these particular rooms will have smooth ceilings is because the accoustical material does not stand up well in a possible moisture laden atmosphere. Kitchens, bathrooms, powder room and laundry area definitely fall into the category of rooms which are subject to high levels of moisture or humidity.

Look at the ceilings in these rooms to be sure that they are perfectly smooth and that no nail holes or joints are visible. If you see any small lumps in the surface, they are probably what are called "nail pops": a nail has worked loose but has not yet broken through the surface of the drywall material.

The drywall is installed in large sheets and is nailed to the studs or frame of the wall. Therefore, the obvious things to look for are that the nail depressions are covered and that the joints where the sheets of drywall meet are smooth. When you can't see the joints, it's a good job! Again, as in the ceiling inspection, look for those "nail pops."

By the time you conduct your walk-through, the walls will have been painted which will tend to show up the defects and make your inspection job easier. As we mentioned before, the entire surface should be smooth unless, of course, the walls are textured. If they are textured, the surface should be uniform and not have any blank or heavy spots in the texture pattern.

Be sure to look at all the electrical outlets, wall switches, TV and telephone outlets to make certain that the cover plates do, in fact, cover the hole made in the drywall for the installation of the switch or outlet. If the plate does not cover the hole, it means that the drywall installer has made the hole too large. This is a fairly common problem which is easily repaired and you should insist that it be done.

Be certain to look carefully inside all of the closets, behind the doors and inside of cabinets to see that all the drywall has really been installed and that it is textured to match the rest of the wall area.

Don't forget to ask your builder's representative for the brand and number of the paint that was used on both the interior and exterior of the house. This will enable you to buy paint later on for touch up work.

17

5

HALLWAYS AND STAIRWELLS

Most of us don't pay too much attention to hallways and stairwells. This is probably because we tend to think of these areas as only leading to or from another room or to go up or down the stairs to another level of the house.

Be sure to examine these two areas just as closely as you would the living room, bedroom or any other room. Check the ceilings and walls just as you did in the other rooms. These two areas are even more prone to accidental damage by the workmen than is the rest of the house. This is because all of the finish materials have to be carried through these areas to get to any other room in the house.

When you are inspecting the stairwell(s), grasp the handrails firmly and check for sturdiness. They must provide adequate support in assisting someone up or down the stairs. Therefore, make sure that whether they are made of wood, wrought iron, brass or chrome that they are securely fastened to either the wall or the floor.

While we are on the subject of stairwells, carefully check the stairway steps for SQUEAKS. If at all possible, try to get to inspect them before the carpeting has been installed. It makes it easier to locate the squeak when the carpet is not in the way.

There is only one way to properly inspect the stairs for squeaks: one step at a time! Beginning with the bottom step, walk up the stairs, stopping on each step to put your weight first on the left side, then on the right and last in the middle. When you are satisfied that the first step is OK, go on to the second step, etc, until you have checked them all.

Each time you find a squeaky step, make a note as to which step it is and whether the noise comes from the left, right, or center. Give a copy of this note to the customer service person so that the proper squeaky steps can be repaired before the carpet is installed. If your stair carpet is already in place, make your notes as to the location of the squeaks and tell customer service you want them corrected. It is a little more difficult to do when the carpet is down, so it will take a little longer.

Nothing is more irritating then a squeaky step and you will thank me many times over for the peace and quiet!

6

WINDOWS AND DOORS

In these days of rapidly escalating energy costs, proper installation of doors and windows is extremely important. When the doors and windows do not fit properly, air leakage occurs around the top, bottom and sides, allowing drafts and a considerable loss of heating or cooling.

21

WINDOWS

Let's deal first with windows. There are many types that are used in various parts of the country, the choice of which is usually made on the basis of climatic conditions, price and architectural requirements. The types most commonly used, together with a brief description of each, are as follows:

DOUBLE HUNG

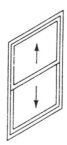

1. **Double hung wood or metal:** A double hung window is one containing two moveable sash sections that slide up and down to provide ventilation both top and bottom.

SLIDING

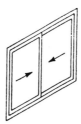

2.   **Sliding window:** Metal or wood, the sliding window contains one or more moveable sash sections which open horizontally.

CASEMENT

22

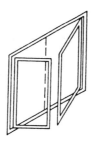

3.   **Casement window:** Can be made of wood or metal. The casement has sash hinged on the sides that swing out somewhat like a door.

JALOUSIE

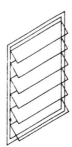

4.   **Jalousie window:** Can be made of a wood or metal frame and has moveable glass slat sections, sloping upward from the outside, somewhat like a venetian blind.

AWNING

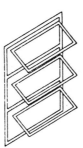

5. **Awning window:** Can be wood or metal. An awning window is one in which the sash or sash sections pivot outward from the top edge, giving an awning effect.

All of the windows described above are normally supplied with insect screens that fit either on the outside or inside of the window depending on the swing or opening direction of the sash.

Storm sash or combination screen and storm sash units are available for these windows and may or not be supplied by your builder as a standard item. Screens are normally supplied in all cases.

23

We will deal next with the problems that can only occur with the metal framed sliding window as this is the one type of residential window that is installed in two stages and not as a completely assembled unit.

CHECK LIST: sliding windows.

1. The sliding window consists of two main parts, the frame and the glass panels. The frame for the window is installed during the framing stage of the building before the interior and exterior wall sheathing is applied. The glass panels are then installed after the house is fully enclosed and the roof is on.

2. If the frames are not installed exactly "square," the resulting "out of square" condition creates problems in the final fitting and operation of the sliding glass portion of the window. When you look at the finished product, with the glass installed,see if the window "looks" square. When square, the sides look exactly vertical and the top and bottom look exactly horizontal.

3. Next, check the operation of the unit. Do the sections slide back and forth easily and do the locks work?

4. Finally, slide the window almost to the closed position to where the frame of the sliding portion is about ¼" from the stationary frame section. Then examine the spacing from the top to bottom. If the space is the same, this indicates that the window is "square."

5.   If there is more space on top than there is at the bottom or vice versa, this means that the frame is "out of square."

Note: if the window is "out of square" so much so that the condition interferes with the operation of the unit, or the window will not close evenly enough to provide a tight seal against wind and drafts, you should insist that the problem be corrected. The builder may try to come up with a multitude of excuses to avoid correcting the problem, because to do so requires major tearing out and repairs to both the inside and outside wall surfaces. STAND FIRM - Insist that it be done!

To avoid this major reconstruction process, it is sometimes possible to get the glass contractor who supplied the windows and frames to remove the glass from the window in question and cut the glass "out of square" and reinstall it in the frame. This will then make the window and glass "out of square" and it will now match the "out of square" frame condition and form a tight seal.

24

DOORS

CHECK LIST:

1.   The first thing to look at when examining doors is if they operate smoothly and effortlessly. Do they latch securely and do the locks work?

2.   When you have checked this to your satisfaction, close the door from the inside and look at the spaces between the door and the frame. This is especially critical on exterior doors where drafts can be a problem and allow loss of heating and cooling.

3.   When the door is closed, check to see that it is not warped. If it does not close tightly and evenly, against the side and top stops, this may indicate warpage in the door. This condition can also be caused by the frame not having been installed correctly. Have the builder decide which problem exists and correct it.

4.   Next, look at the door surfaces both front and back. Check for imperfections such as splitting of the wood or separation of the joints, bubbles or depressions in the skin (veneer surface) and any other cosmetic imperfections or damage. Look at the edges of the door and check to see that the "skin" has not separated from the the main frame portion of the door. If it has, the door is beginning to de-laminate and should be repaired or replaced.

5. When you are conducting your walk-through, the carpeting may not be installed. When a door opens into a room where carpet will be installed, make sure the bottoms of the doors have been cut off to the correct height so that the door will not rub on the surface of the carpet.

    Generally speaking, unless the carpet to be installed is unusually thick, a space of 1¼" to 1½" between the uncarpeted floor and bottom of the door, depending on the thickness of the carpet and padding, will allow sufficient clearance.

6. Where a door is to open onto a floor surface, such as vinyl, tile or wood, make sure that the door has NOT been cut off to the same height as for carpet. If it has been cut for carpet by mistake, you will have an usually large space between the bottom of the door and the floor covering. In that case, you might consider insisting that the door be replaced with one that is cut to the right height from the floor.

7. All exterior doors should have some type of "weather stripping" installed on them to prevent drafts and leakage of heating or cooling. There are many types of weather stripping that can be installed. A simple way to check the effectiveness of the installation is to close the door tightly and see if you can slip a business card between the weather stripping and the door frame. If it is tight all around, chances are that the job was done correctly. If there are still obvious loose areas, have the builder correct this problem.

25

8. Last of all, when examining the doors, check to see that door stops have been installed at all doors. The door stops prevent the door knob from hitting the adjacent wall and causing damage to the wall surface.

7

ELECTRICAL FIXTURES, OUTLETS, ETC.

This is another very important part of the walk-through inspection process that is easily forgotten or overlooked.

Make sure that all of the electrical fixtures are installed. The most obvious ones to look for are ceiling fixtures such as might be used in the dining room, breakfast room or family room areas. Check to see that the fixtures are complete with all the necessary parts such as globes, shades, chimneys, crystals, etc. Many times you will find that the glass parts have been left in their original packing and stored in one of the closets or cabinets for safe keeping.

If you have ordered a special or upgraded dining room or other fixture, make certain that the fixture you ordered is the one that has been installed.

Exterior fixtures should also be checked. These would include a front entry fixture(s), patio fixtures, rear and side entry fixtures. Don't forget the garage. It will probably have an exterior light as well as an interior light or lights.

As you walk from room to room, look to see that all of the switches and outlets have the cover plates installed. This also applies to telephone and TV outlets.

During your walk-through, look to see that light bulbs have been put into the fixtures. If not, ask the builder's representative if bulbs are supplied, or if it is your responsibility. Regardless of whose duty it is, see that they are installed **before** you move in. Your movers may arrive late in the day and it could get mighty dark in the house before any of your lamps are unpacked!

As soon as the electric service has been turned on (this may or may not have happened prior to your walk-through) check all of the three-way switches for proper operation. Three-way switches are usually found in kitchens, family room, living room, dining room , hallways and stairwells.

If you are not familiar with the term "Three-Way," it means that the system was wired so that a fixture can be turned on or off from two locations. You will usually find them in the rooms mentioned above because they might have more than one entrance or exit. With switches located at both entrances, you can turn the light on when you enter and turn it off from another doorway as you exit.

An easy way to tell if a wall switch is "Three-Way" is to look at the toggle part of the switch (the part that moves up and down). If it doesn't have "on" or "off" molded into the plastic toggle, it is a three-way switch. The switches that indicate "on" and "off" are what are called single-pole switches and will operate the fixture or outlet from that one location.

Here's another tip that may save you a service call after you move in. Most electrical codes and regulations now require that in every room that does not have a ceiling fixture, a wall switch must be installed that will operate one part of one of the wall outlets. This regulation was enacted for safety reasons. With a lamp connected to the "switched outlet," you can turn on the light before entering a dark room without having to stumble around feeling for the lamp switch.

To determine which outlet is "switched", turn the wall switch to the OFF position and then plug a small lamp or tester into each outlet both top and bottom. When you find the one outlet, either top or bottom, that does not turn on the lamp or tester, that one is the "switched outlet."

You might want to locate these "switched outlets" before moving your furniture in as their location might influence your decision as to where you want to place table lamps, etc. This "switched outlet" is normally only one half of the outlet, either top or bottom. This is done so that the other half of the outlet will be ON at all times, so that you can use an electric clock or electric blanket, for example.

Should you find that both sockets in the "switched outlet" go ON and OFF with the switch, make a note to have the electrician repair this "goof."

In one of the bathrooms, you may notice a strange looking electrical outlet that has, in addition to the two plug receptacles, two buttons marked "test" and "reset." This is called a GFI outlet (GROUND FAULT INTERRUPTER), which is required in many jurisdictions and listed in most electrical codes.

It's purpose is as follows: when any appliance such as an electric razor, hair dryer, curling iron, or radio is plugged into this outlet and if there should be the slightest, most miniscule short circuit, or should the appliance be dropped into a sink, bath tub, or toilet full of water, the outlet will immediately trip and cut off electricity to the outlet. This safety device will prevent the possibility of electrocution or serious injury to the user. If installed correctly, this outlet should be wired on a separate circuit that includes the outlets in all bathrooms and all outlets on the exterior of the house.

Even though you only see one outlet of this type, the remaining outlets on this circuit will be protected by the one GFI outlet.

28

A simple way to test the wiring of this important circuit is as follows:

Press the "test" button. This will trip the outlet and shut off the power to the circuit. With the power off, plug a small tester or light into each of the other bath and exterior outlets to see that they are also off. If they are, the circuit is wired correctly. If any of them are "hot," note this on your walk-through sheet to have the electrician correct the problem.

After you have performed the test, press the "reset" button to re-activate the circuit.

It is possible that the electrician may have installed a GFI circuit breaker in the electrical panel instead of using a GFI outlet in one of the bathrooms. If this is the case, it is perfectly OK since it will provide the same degree of safety. The testing procedure for this is essentially the same: trip the breaker at the electrical panel and then see if any of the exterior or bathroom outlets are "hot".

29

8

THE DECORATING CENTER EXPERIENCE

If the home you are buying is being built in a fairly large tract, shortly after construction commences, you will be asked to visit the Decorating Center. There you will be asked to make your decisions from the selections offered by the builder as "standard equipment." At this time, you will choose the colors and styles you want in such items as ceramic tile, Formica counter tops, carpeting, draperies, resilient floor coverings, etc.

You will then be shown these same items in what your builder is offering in the better and best quality to encourage you to "upgrade" all of your floor coverings, tile, counter tops, etc. at additional cost.

Depending on the builder, you may also be offered the option of paying extra for upgraded appliances: stove, dishwasher, refrigerator, trash compactor, garage door opener, gas barbecues, etc.

Therefore, you will be well advised to be ready with a firm budgeted dollar amount which you will not exceed for all of these items. It is very easy in the excitement of the moment to take on more expenses than you financially can handle. Remember that many of these items can be upgraded after you have been living in the house for some months.

If finances are tight for you at this time but there are items that you want to upgrade, you should choose only the things that are more economical to do while the house is under construction.

A prime example of this would be the addition of a patio or the enclosing of the standard open patio. It would obviously be cheaper to do this while construction is in process rather than have to call the contractor back after the house is completed.

Here's another money saving idea that you might want to consider: if you now own appliances such as a washer, dryer and refrigerator that are in good to excellent condition and, if any of these items are part of the package supplied with your house, you may want to investigate how much credit you will be allowed if you use your present appliances.

Assuming that you may need to make a decision as to whether you want to use your present appliances or sell them and use the ones supplied by the builder, below is the U.S. Department of Energy chart of the average life expectancy of major appliances:

	years
Dehumidifiers	11
Dishwashers	12
Dryers	18½
Freezers	21
Ranges & Ovens	18
Refrigerators	19
Washers	13

To summarize: This is a time when you might tend to go overboard in your purchasing. Buying a home is a very emotional experience and it is easy to allow yourself to get carried away in the emotion of the moment. It might be wiser for you to select only the basics necessary for occupancy and to add the other items after you have lived in the house for a while. You may find that your needs change and you could be sorry that you purchased the wrong items or the wrong color or quality.

Remember, the people at the Decorating Center earn the major portion of their livelihood based upon how much they can sell you over and above the standard items which are included in the original purchase price. So, if you are not a prudent and careful shopper, you may be shocked to find your house cost escalating out of sight of your original budget.

Above all and most importantly, no matter what you select or purchase BE SURE YOU GET A COPY IN WRITING OF ALL YOUR SELECTIONS AND PURCHASES and make sure it is dated and signed by you and the builder's decorator representative.

This will avoid all sorts of possible problems down the road if, by chance, the wrong items or the wrong color appliance is installed in your home or if your walls were painted blue instead of pink! Armed with a copy of your selection sheet, the builder has no choice but to correct the error.

9

THE GARAGE, ATTIC AND BASEMENT

Probably one of the most hurried examinations, done by most new home buyers, is of the garage. Usually, just a few cursory glances are given to satisfy your curiosity that a garage, does in fact, exist!. However, there are several things to inspect that may turn out to be very important to you after you occupy your new home.

Check to see that all doors, including any side or rear doors, operate smoothly and with little effort. Also try all the locks to make sure that they work properly.

If the main entrance door(s) has an electric garage door opener, check to see that it operates smoothly and that the door(s) doesn't bind at the top, bottom or sides. Also, be sure that the builder gives you the remote control units that will operate the opener from your car. Open and close the door with the remote unit to make sure that you were given the unit that is tuned to the frequency of your door opener.

Should there not be an electric opener, check to see if the builder has installed a 110 volt electrical outlet in the ceiling area to accomodate the installation of an opener at a later date. If none is there, you may want to have the builder's electrician install one for you. It will probably be less expensive to have it done while the electrician is still on the job.

Next, look at the garage floor. If your garage is attached to the house, the surface of the floor should be at least four inches below the first floor level of the house. This will be a safety barrier to prevent any water that gets into the garage from entering the main part of the house.

After you have checked the height of the floor, look at the surface of the floor itself. It should be smooth, free of cracks and have a slight pitch toward the main entrance doors. This pitch will encourage any standing water to flow out the front of the garage and not "puddle" on the floor.

Any garage walls and ceilings that are common to, or back up to, interior walls or ceilings, should be finished with drywall or plaster so that there are no openings. This is not only to prevent drafts, but will also afford a protective fire barrier from the rest of the house. This probably has been done as most standard building codes require that these common walls be sealed.

You will probably also notice two or more ventilation holes about 5 inches high and 10 inches wide, just a few inches above the floor level on a side or rear wall. These are installed in ground level garages to provide ventilation so that any raw gasoline fumes can escape. If your gas fired hot water heater is located in the garage, these ventilation holes will also provide the necessary combustion air for the gas heater. The main thing for you to check here is to see that these holes have screen wire installed in them no larger than ¼ inch mesh. This wire mesh, called "bird screen," will keep small rodents, neighborhood cats and small dogs out of your garage.

34

THE ATTIC

UNIFORM BUILDING CODE, published by International Conference of Building Officials, Whittier, CA, sets forth model codes used by most governmental building departments. In a section covering attic spaces, it states that "a readily accessible attic access opening is required of not less than 22 inches by 30 inches to be provided to any attic area having a clear height of over 30 inches."

The attic in your new house may range anywhere from this basic requirement to a finished stairway leading up to a large area that may be utilized for storage or converted to additional living quarters in the future.

In any case, the attic is the one area in the house that can be inspected that will show you the type of insulation that has been provided. You can see the thickness, at least, in the ceiling area, but at this stage, all the side walls will be sealed so that you will not be able to determine the thickness used there.

Be sure that your builder's representative gives you the insulation installation certificate supplied by his insulation sub-contractor. This will certify the type of insulation that has been installed in the house and what are the "R" values (see GLOSSARY for definition of "R" value).

If your house is being financed through either FHA or VA, this insulation certificate will be required by their inspectors.

If your attic access is by means of a hatch opening in a ceiling, be sure to check that the top side of the hatch cover (the side facing the roof) has been insulated. A cover that has not been insulated could result in a considerable amount of heat loss in a year's time.

When your attic entry is by means of a pull-down stairway or a permanently installed staircase, be sure to see that the stairs are sturdy and that some sort of handrail is provided for safety.

During your inspection of the unfinished attic space, be sure to check to see that ventilation openings have been provided and are covered by wire screen with a mesh opening of not more than ¼ inch. These openings are important as they dissipate heat build-up in the summer as well as provide the circulation of air the year round.

THE BASEMENT

If your house has a basement, the first thought that comes to everyone's mind is: is it dry? I have lived with basements that got wet and I know how aggravating that condition can be.

I have no magical advice to give you so that you can determine, during your walk-through, whether your basement will be a "leaker" or not. The logical things to inspect are the basement walls and floors to see that no major cracks have developed and to look for any water stains on the concrete which might indicate that there may have been a leak. Make notes of any of these abnormalities on your walk-through sheet.

Ask your builder's representative if the warranty on the house extends to, and covers, the basement for water leakage. If it does, you will have some consolation in the fact that at least you have someone to turn to if this problem develops.

As with stairs leading to the attic, the same applies to stairways to the basement area. Make sure the stairs are sturdy and that proper handrails have been installed. The stairs need not be fancy, but should be serviceable and safe. Keep in mind that should you decide to add a recreation room in your basement, the plain set of stairs can be removed and replaced with a finished staircase for a better appearance.

10

THE EXTERIOR

The first item of importance to look at on the outside of the house is the structure itself.

If the exterior is stucco, look for cracks in the stucco coating. Minor hairline cracks are to be expected and are considered normal. However, be wary of cracks in the stucco that are any wider than ⅛ inch and you should insist that they be repaired. Also check to see that the texture and color of the stucco is consistent.

If the house is brick, make sure that the brick appears to be symmetrical. That is, the brick courses or lines should look level and the mortar joints should be of equal size. Look for any cracks in the mortar joints between the bricks. A brick wall will not usually crack directly through one of the bricks, but the crack will follow the course of least resistance: the joints.

On a house with wood siding, again look for uniformity. Whether the siding is wood shingle, beveled wood siding, board and batten, or plywood paneling, all joint lines should be straight and properly joined. If the siding is stained or painted, see that the color is uniform throughout.

There should be caulking or sealant material wherever different materials meet: wood to stucco, wood to brick, window frames, door frames and patio door frames. There should be some type of sealant material used wherever anything comes through the walls or roof such as electrical conduits, air conditioning lines, water or gas lines, plumbing vents, heater and furnace vents, etc. In addition, the head (top) of the windows and doors need flashing to keep water from finding its way behind the frames and inside the wall cavity.

Exterior doors should be weather-stripped on the side edges as well as top and bottom. If you can see daylight around, over or under a door or you can feel a draft around the closed door, it has not been weather-stripped properly. The types of weather stripping vary as to the climate in your particular area. In the sun belt states you will find very simple forms of weather stripping such as peel and stick sponge rubber and vinyl bumper strip against which the door closes.

The type of weather stripping changes from this simple type to the kind found in more severe cold climates such as the northeast states, nothern midwest and Alaska. There you will undoubtedly find an interlocking metal type of weather stripping used. No matter which type is used in your house, the main purpose of the weather stripping is to stop drafts coming through around the edges of the doorways.

Next look at the fascia boards. Make sure that they are not cracked or twisted and see that any joints are tight and evenly cut and matched.

Up near the roof line you will probably see some ventilation holes or metal grilles. Make sure they have bird screen (discussed in the last chapter) installed in them, as they will prevent birds, rodents and large insects from entering the roof attic area.

If your house has a basement and if there are windows in the basement, make sure that the basement window wells have beds of gravel and not just a dirt base. The gravel should be of sufficient thickness to allow accumulated water to drain out and not fill up the well and leak in the window.

Check that the yard is graded so that it slopes away from the foundation or footing so that you will have the proper drainage for rain water or the water from melting snow. The grade slope should be sufficient so that the water will flow out into the street or to a drain system that eventually flows to the street or into a storm sewer. If the property is not graded properly, you could eventually have water problems in the basement or crawl space area. Even if your house has no basement and is built on a concrete slab, the water should still drain away from the house.

In addition to the grading, the earth itself should be firm and settled solidly and not graded too high around the exterior walls. Six to eight inches of foundation or footing wall should be showing between the ground level and the first floor level. This spacing, together with chemical treatment of the soil in some areas, will prevent termites and other wood boring insects from entering the first floor framing lumber.

Walkways and driveways should also slope away from the house for obvious reasons. If the roof downspouts (drain pipes) are not piped to the street or storm sewer, there should be splash blocks placed under their outlets to carry the water away from the house.

This, of course, does not apply if your house is below street level. If that is the case, there will be other provisions made to keep the water away from the house by diverting it into drain channels which will carry it to a lower area.

Check for any standing water under and around patios, walkways and driveways. If there is evidence of standing water, you can expect the concrete to eventually settle and crack in those areas.

Next, visually examine the roof. The shingles should be flat and not curled or torn. This, of course only applies to asphalt or composition shingles. If your house has wood shingles or shakes or clay or cement tile roofing material, look to see that it appears to be uniformly installed. The lines where the materials overlap should be

38

straight and even. Check the best you can from your ground level position to see that the roof flashings, chimneys and vent pipes are properly sealed.

After you have looked carefully at the roof, check to see that gutters and downspouts have been installed. The ideal situation is to have enough gutters and downspouts placed to catch and carry away rain water from every area of the roof. Based upon climatic or economic considerations, your builder may have only installed these items at strategic points or he may not have installed any at all. If your house is in a development, compare your house with the model. If your house is custom built, check your plans and specifications to see that what is installed conforms to the them.

If your house is financed through a U.S. Government insured loan, such as VA or FHA, they require that the roof water be diverted away from areas above all exterior entry doorways.

Last, examine all sidewalks, walkways and patio floors. These surfaces will, no doubt, be made of asphalt or poured concrete. If they are concrete, check for cracks in the slab surface and for broken corners. Broken or cracked corners are a common problem on large sites and are caused by heavy trucks or construction equipment driving over the surfaces after they have been installed.

If the paving is asphalt, check to see that it is level and free of humps, dips and depressions.

Whether they are asphalt or concrete, look to see that they appear to be pitched in the right direction so that any water will not only drain off the surface but also away from the house.

39

LANDSCAPING

Even though landscaping is an integral part of the appearance of your new house, it is a subject that we will deal with here only from the overall aspect. There are so many different climates, soil conditions and varieties of plantings native to specific areas of this great country of ours, it is impossible to deal in anything but generalities.

The only real practical advice that can be given is to check your contract with your builder to see if landscaping is included in the package and then make sure that everything specified in your agreement to be installed or planted, is done.

Many builders only plant grass seed in the front yard area. Others may landscape the entire property while a few may supply nothing in the way of ground cover or plantings.

If you are buying a condominium, the exterior landscaping, irrigation, plantings and the maintenance is contracted for by your homeowner's association. The monthly dues of your homeowner's association then covers the cost of these services as well as maintenance of the outside of the buildings.

11

SECURITY AND SAFETY

Whether your house is being built in a tract, subdivision or individually custom built, there comes a time during the course of construction when the windows and exterior doors and locks are installed. After this stage is completed, the unit is considered to be "closed in."

DOORS

At this point it becomes necessary for the job superintendent and the foremen of the various trades to have easy access to the house. The superintendent will pass out "builder's" keys to these people who need access.

Most major lock manufacturers have devised and built into their locks a system that generally works as follows:

1. The manufacturer delivers all of the locks for the project to the job superintendent packaged and marked for each house or unit together with a supply of "builder's" keys and a few "master" keys.

2. When the finish carpenters have installed the locks for your particular house, they will deliver the package of keys to the superintendent for delivery to you when you move in.

3. At this point, the keys for your house will only open the locks on your house, but the "builder's" and "master" keys will open all of the locks in all of the houses.

4. When you are ready to move in, the superintendent, or representative, will insert a special "knockout" key into each lock. This "knockout" key, when inserted into the lock, pushes the last tumbler in the lock out of position which now makes the "builder's" key inoperable. The system that accomplishes this "knockout" operation may vary from one manufacturer to another, but the result is the same.

5.   When this has been accomplished, only your keys will be the ones that will open your doors EXCEPT for the "master" which the superintendent has.

After you have moved in, you will have a reasonable sense of security in knowing that, theoretically, the only other person who has access to your home is the job superintendent.

When the corrective work has been completed (those items that were spelled out on your walk through sheets) you might want to consider having a locksmith come out to your house and remove the master tumblers from your exterior locks. This will then make the "master" key inoperable and now YOU will have the only keys that open your locks, and the construction people will no longer have access.

Check with your builder to see if the locks used are of the type described above. If not, you most certainly should have a locksmith come out after the corrective work is completed and re-key your locks so that only you have access.

In most areas of the country where building codes are in effect and enforced, dead bolts are required to be installed on all exterior doors. Since most "crimes of opportunity" come right through the front and back doors, these dead bolts are the cheapest form of insurance that can be provided.

42

Below are shown and described the two types of dead bolts:

SINGLE CYLINDER DEAD BOLT

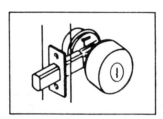

The single cylinder dead bolt is one that requires a key to open it from the outside, but only a twist of the thumbscrew to open it from the inside. The main advantage to this type of dead bolt is fire safety. Since you don't need a key, it is easy to open if you have to get out of the house in a hurry.

DOUBLE CYLINDER DEAD BOLT

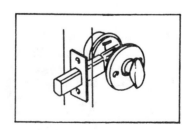

The double cylinder dead bolt requires a key in order to open it from either inside or outside. This type of lock is required in many jurisdictions under certain circumstances. For example, they are mandatory if the door has a glass insert or if there is a window within 40 inches of the dead bolt. This is to prevent an unauthorized person from gaining access to the house by breaking the glass and reaching in to open the lock.

If your house has any exterior doors that open outward, this means that the door hinges are exposed to the outside. These hinges may need immediate special attention! All a burglar has to do is to remove the hinge pins and your locked, dead bolted door can be merely lifted away. For a very nominal amount, you can protect your house from this simple means of intrusion:

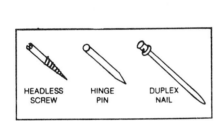

HEADLESS SCREW   HINGE PIN   DUPLEX NAIL

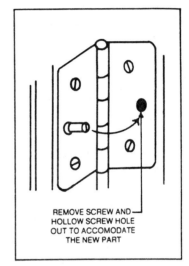

REMOVE SCREW AND HOLLOW SCREW HOLE OUT TO ACCOMODATE THE NEW PART

43

To remedy this problem, take one of the center screws out of each hinge and install a headless screw, a hingepin or a duplex nail into the empty screw hole. Next remove the corresponding screw from the other leaf of the hinge so that the door can now close onto the new exposed pin. When this is done, the door can't be lifted off the hinges.

VISUAL SURVEILLANCE

All exterior doors should have some sort of viewing device or "peephole." Inexpensive and easy to install, one will enable you to see who is outside before you open the door and violate your own security. You might consider installing two peepholes in each door; one at standard height, and another lower one for young children and short adults.

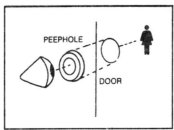

PEEPHOLE   DOOR

GLASS DOORS AND WINDOWS

Glass doors can be another problem area for the security-conscious homeowner since some of these doors can literally be lifted right out of their tracks even when the door is locked. Putting a broom stick or piece of wood in the bottom track won't solve the problem. It's easy for a burglar using a flat piece of metal to wedge it between the glass doors and pick the broom handle out of the track.

There are two ways to discourage uninvited entry:

1.   Since it is easy to lift the door out of its track, install sliding door anti-lift plates. These are relatively inexpensive, easy to install and fit snugly into the upper track of the sliding door to prevent lift out. They are removeable if you need to work on the door, but once they are installed neither you nor an intruder can lift the door out of its track.

2.   Buy a sliding glass door lock. The best locks have keys; the less expensive ones have a metal pin that is installed through the door frame and track. However, if a burglar cuts away a piece of glass, it is easy for him to pull the pin and open the door.

44

The same kinds of locks and anti-lift devices are also available for sliding glass windows, and we recommend that you purchase and install them in at least your first floor windows.

Most window and door manufacturers supply the anti-lift devices with their windows. Check to see that they have been installed and, if not, ask your builder's representative if they are normally supplied as a standard item.

Proper window security depends upon the type of window you have.

Here's how to solve the problem with other types of windows:

If you have French windows (windows that open like two double doors) a simple catch, fastening the two windows together is not at all adequate. You must also install slide bolts or slide locks toward the center corners of the window, top and bottom.

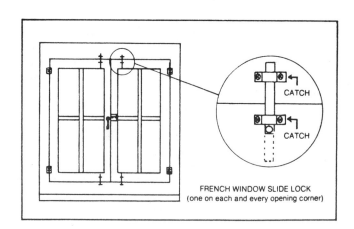

FRENCH WINDOW SLIDE LOCK
(one on each and every opening corner)

Many houses have the vertical sliding metal or wood windows (double hung) with a semi-circular catch lock in the middle of the window. But again, all a burglar has to do is cut away only a small part of the glass, reach in and flip the latch open.

Three ways to protect double hung windows are:

1. Install window locks with keys. The cost is nominal. The best systems have two positions; one to close the window completely, and the other to permit the locked window to remain slightly open to allow for ventilation. See FIGURE A below.

2. A more economical approach is to drive a nail or put a screw into the window track to prevent it from being lifted. See CENTER FIGURE below.

3. Drill a hole into the window sash (FIGURE C) through to the other sash. Then you simply insert a rod, nail or commercial window pin to keep the window from being opened from outside.

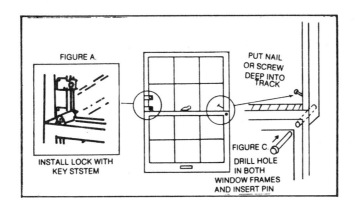

45

One of the best deterrents against burglars is a well lighted house both inside and especially outside. If a view of your house is obscured by bushes or trees, this permits more privacy to a burglar who is attempting a break-in.

Good exterior lighting from multi-directional flood lights will discourage burglars from trying to enter your house.

Here are some of the most important DOs and DON'Ts that you need to know to prevent break-ins.

DON'T EVER leave door keys under mats, rocks, over sills or any place where someone who knows all the tricks would eventually find them. Law enforcement officials know that experienced burglars always look for keys first.

DO make sure to arrange for someone to pick up your mail, newspapers, packages, or other deliveries, when you plan to be away for more than one day.

DON'T EVER leave a note on the door for a friend telling that you are away and when you will return.

DO get to know your neighbors and agree to watch each other's homes. This is an accepted practice in some parts of the country where NEIGHBORHOOD WATCH, a proven crime deterrent, is in effect.

DON'T EVER leave your house, even "for just a minute," without securing it. Many victims tell police "But, I was only gone for a few minutes." Some burglars specialize in this type of theft.

DO tell your close neighbors as well as your friends and relatives who live nearby when you will be gone for a period of time and arrange for one of them to check out your house on a regular basis.

DO record the license number, make and model of any suspicious or unknown vehicles that appear in your neighborhood. Then, if a problem occurs, you can give police the information to follow up.

DON'T EVER be afraid to phone police if someone or something in your neighborhood seems suspicious. Often when investigating crimes, police are told by neighbors that they noticed unusual things and failed to call police. The police WANT you to call them.

The task of crime prevention cannot be accomplished by the police department alone. It requires the willing cooperation of both the police and the public, working together toward a common goal.

DO always be suspicious of:

    . Any UNKNOWN person.

    . Any young person or adult "selling" anything door-to-door.

    . Anyone taking a "shortcut" through your yard.

    . Any visitor or repairman hanging around your neighbor's house if you know the neighbor is not at home.

    . Anyone acting suspiciously, especially if that person is just hanging around.

FIRE SAFETY

Special thanks is given to The Los Angeles Fire Department for the following suggestions for fire safety for residential houses. Read them over carefully and, if you have any questions, contact your own fire department who will be happy to answer your questions. They might even offer additional advice and suggestions for your particular geographical area.

HAVE AN ESCAPE PLAN

Review layout of rooms; where possible, have two exits. DO NOT have a cluttered hallway.

Plan an assembly place for your family to meet outside, so you can quickly determine who is missing and inform firefighters when they arrive. DO NOT attempt to re-enter the burning house.

Schools have fire drills to protect your children. Why not insure the safety of your entire family by conducting a fire drill in your home twice a year?

When exiting from the second floor, use ladders, your garage or porch roof and, if necessary, trees.

Keep bedroom doors closed while asleep. This is especially important in a two story house.

Leave at the first indication of a fire!

Remember: Phone the fire department or 911, if this number is functional in your area. Make certain they are called! It is surprising how often there is a delay in reporting a fire.

CHECK THE DOORS AND WINDOWS

Can doors exiting to the outside be opened without the aid of a key? Are they easily opened? Sticking doors could jamb shut, trapping you in a fire.

47

Latches and chains on the doors are good for security,but if they are positioned up high, could they be found in a dark, hot, smokey atmosphere? Would they be especially difficult for children to unlatch?

Can windows be easily opened? Check and make sure.

Are the window openings large enough for an adult to leave through? Check the opening for ease of escape — it may surprise you.

Are bushes and trees a hindrance to your departure? Rosebushes and other thorny plants can create havoc during your escape.

Decorative security grilles or bars can keep burglars out, but they also can trap you inside during a fire. Such security grilles must be open-able from inside without the aid of a key or special tool.

SMOKE DETECTORS

Smoke detectors are required by many city ordinances to be installed in each bedroom or sleeping area and also in all areas (such as hallways) giving access to the bedrooms and sleeping areas. The portion of the ordinance that applies to single-family dwellings, in Los Angeles county, is as follows:

"Permanently wired smoke detectors connected to the electrical wiring of the dwelling shall be installed in each sleeping room and in the area giving access to any such room."

TYPICAL SMOKE DETECTOR PLACEMENT
(Required by Los Angeles Municipal Code)

SINGLE
CEILING MOUNTED

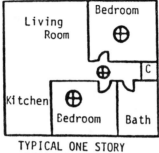

TYPICAL ONE STORY
CEILING MOUNTED

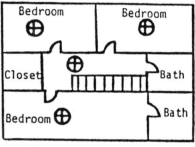

TYPICAL SECOND FLOOR
CEILING MOUNTED

48

⊕ SMOKE DETECTOR

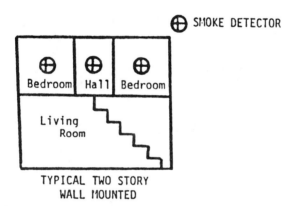

TYPICAL TWO STORY
WALL MOUNTED

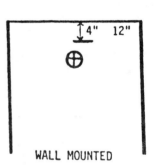

WALL MOUNTED

Smoke detectors shall be installed at a point centrally located on the wall or ceiling, in every sleeping room and in each hallway, corridor, or adjacent area to any such sleeping room. Where sleeping rooms are on an upper level, a detector shall be placed at the center of the ceiling directly above the stairway.

The top of any smoke detector installed on a wall shall be on closer than four inches to the ceiling and no farther than 12 inches.

In bachelor or efficiency units, one smoke detector shall be centrally mounted on the ceiling or wall.

If you live in an area that is vulnerable to brush or forest fires, see the chart on the following page for guidance as to how to protect your house from those catastrophies.

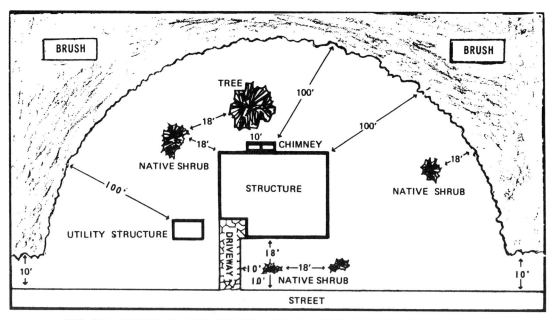

CUT ALL BRUSH TO THE GROUND BUT DO NOT DISTURB ROOT SYSTEM WITHIN THE CIRCLE AND ALONG THE ROAD

49

NEW BRUSH CLEARANCE LAW

A FIREMAN, WHO MUST TRY TO PROTECT YOUR HOME FROM A BRUSH FIRE, WOULD LIKE EVERY ADVANTAGE HE CAN GET. HE WOULD LIKE TO SEE EVERY BIT OF HAZARDOUS VEGETATION CLEARED AWAY, RIGHT DOWN TO THE BARE EARTH.

THE HOMEOWNER, ON THE OTHER HAND, APPRECIATES THE BEAUTY OF THE BRUSH AND ENJOYS THE RUSTIC SECLUSION IT OFFERS.

THEY BOTH REALIZE THE DANGER FROM FLOODS AND EARTH-SLIDES THAT MIGHT RESULT FROM A BARREN HILLSIDE.

RESULT: A REASONABLE LAW.

HOW IT WORKS

REDUCE THE AMOUNT OF NATIVE BRUSH TO A POINT WHERE FIREMEN WILL STAND A GOOD CHANCE OF SAVING YOUR HOME IN THE EVENT OF A FIRE.

TO MAKE YOUR HOME AS SAFE AS POSSIBLE WITHOUT DESTROYING THE BEAUTY OF ITS SETTING THE LOS ANGELES CITY FIRE CODE REQUIRES THE FOLLOWING:

IN THE "NATIVE BRUSH" AROUND YOUR HOME

1. REMOVE NATIVE BRUSH AND OTHER HAZARDOUS VEGETATION FOR A DISTANCE OF 100 FEET AROUND ALL STRUCTURES AND 10 FEET FROM THE SIDES OF ROADS AND DRIVEWAYS THAT ARE USED BY MORE THAN ONE RESIDENCE.
   EXCEPTION: YOU MAY RETAIN "SPECIMEN NATIVE SHRUBS" IF THEY ARE TRIMMED 2 FEET ABOVE GROUND, DO NOT EXCEED APPROXIMATELY 7 FEET IN DIAMETER, ARE MAINTAINED FREE OF ALL DEAD WOOD, DUFF, DRY LEAVES AND ARE NOT CLOSER TOGETHER THAN 18 FEET AIR SPACE.
2. IT IS A GOOD IDEA TO HAVE A REGULAR WATERING PROGRAM.

IN AND AROUND YOUR HOUSE AND GARAGE

1. ALLOW NO TREES, SHRUBS OR OTHER VEGETATION TO GROW WITHIN 10 FEET OF THE OUTLET OF ANY CHIMNEY.
2. ALL TREES, SHRUBS, BUSHES OR OTHER VEGETATION ADJACENT TO OR OVERHANGING ANY STRUCTURE MUST BE KEPT FREE OF DEAD LIMBS, BRANCHES AND OTHER COMBUSTIBLE MATTER.
3. KEEP YOUR ROOF AND RAIN GUTTERS FREE OF DEAD LEAVES, NEEDLES, TWIGS AND OTHER COMBUSTIBLE MATTER.
4. KEEP ALL COMBUSTIBLE RUBBISH IN NON-COMBUSTIBLE RUBBISH CONTAINERS WITH TIGHT FITTING LIDS.
5. STACK YOUR WOOD PILE NEATLY AND COMPACTLY IN A LOCATION REMOTE FROM THE HOUSE AND GARAGE, 18 INCHES OFF THE GROUND.

ABOUT FIREPLACES

If your new house has a fireplace, there are two important things to check: the first thing is to make sure that a chimney cap and spark arrestor have been installed on the top of the chimney. The purpose of the spark arrestor is to prevent burning embers from escaping out of the chimney and possibly setting fire to your wood roof or to the surrounding shrubbery. The chimney cap helps to eliminate downdrafts and also prevents water from going down the chimney.

The illustrations below show the chimney cap and spark arrestor separately. It is possible that your builder may have used a combination cap and arrestor. This is fine because it accomplishes both jobs with one unit.

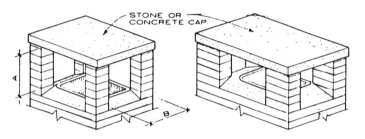

SPARK ARRESTOR

50

Chimney hoods to prevent downdraft due to adjoining hills, buildings, trees, etc.

A should be ¼ greater than B in all hooded chimneys

The second thing is to see that your fireplace has a chimney damper and to check its operation. The damper (illustrated below) serves a very important function when your fireplace is not in use: it closes the chimney so that heat from the house is not dissipated and wasted by going up the chimney.

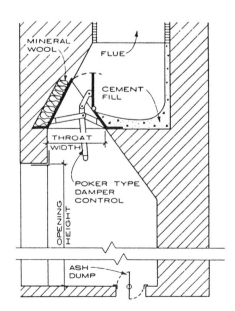

For safety reasons, it is advisable to have your chimney cleaned and inspected by a professional chimney sweep after the burning of two to three cords of wood. It is amazing how many homeowners never think to have the chimney cleaned periodically. These cleanings will not only prevent chimney fires, but when a chimney is clean, it eliminates much household dust.

To have the job done correctly, look in your telephone Yellow Pages under CHIMNEY CLEANING & REPAIRING and choose the professional who is a member of National Chimney Sweep Guild. You may also write to this association at P.O. Box 1078, Merrimack, NH, 03054-1078, or phone them at 603-424-2394, and ask for the name of the member nearest to you.

MAKE YOUR KITCHEN & BATH CHILD-SAFE

Most at-home accidents occur in the kitchen or bath, and many of these involve infants and children. The following guidelines will help prevent these incidents.

Unplug small appliances when they're not in use, so they can't be turned on. Hair-dryers and curling irons can be especially dangerous as well as the blades of food processors, blenders and juicers.

51

Don't let appliance cords dangle over countertops within the child's reach.

Cook on the back burners of the range whenever possible. Keep pot handles turned toward the back and keep the oven door tightly closed.

Dishwashing detergent is a toxic substance. Never add it until you are ready to start the dishwasher.

Place toxic cleaning products used in kitchen and bath in the upper cabinets. If you must keep them under the counter, lock both the kitchen and bath cabinets with easy-to-install childproof latches. These are available at most hardware and home improvement centers.

Cover electrical outlets with safety caps, dummy plugs, or tape to shield them from your child's exploring fingers.

Keep trash baskets and pet dishes out of children's reach. Place empty containers from toxic substances in a covered outside trash can immediately.

Keep all prescription and non-prescription drug items locked up or in a high cabinet that is not accessible to the child. A good time to start teaching your children good kitchen and bath safety habits is right now even before you move into your new house.

IMPORTANT INFORMATION FOR HOMEOWNERS

INSURANCE COVERAGE

The subject of insurance coverage is another facet of the pending ownership of your new house which requires considerable thought and advice. Don't wait until the day before you take title to your property to make a hasty decision as to the amounts of coverage needed.

Get together with your insurance agent or broker in plenty of time so that you and he or she can discuss the items and the coverage needed.

You will, no doubt, purchase what the insurance industry refers to as a HOMEOWNERS POLICY which is an all inclusive policy that can be tailored to your particular requirements. These policies cover the following basic categories of possible losses:

1. The dwelling.
2. The contents (personal property)
3. Personal liability

The often heard warning that your policy must cover the FULL replacement value of your house should not be taken lightly. Most homeowners only discover their coverage is inadequate after a disaster. The true replacement value must be reflected in the original appraisal. Otherwise, there could be many unnecessary heartaches in the already distressing aftermath of a fire, break-in, or other loss.

Only when the claims of the insured are calculated does it become clear that that home's custom features were overlooked in the orginial insurance appraisal.

This author asked John DeNegre, spokesman for the Chubb Group of Insurance Companies' Personal Lines Division, to offer advice from experience based on the company's 100 years in covering upscale residences and valuable articles.

In discussing homes worth $200,000 and up, he explains that many factors in addition to the amount of floor space, general condition and purchase price should figure in insurance appraisal.

"Conventional appraisals ignore many of the most important custom features," DeNegre says. "Too often, the niceties that make a fine home unique are missed during routine insurance appraisals."

"In upscale homes, the true replacement value can be far different from market value or purchase price. Replacement value is the cost, today, of replacing your home or restoring it to its original condition after a loss. Unfortunately, many homeowners don't realize this difference. It's possible for a replacement value to run 40 percent higher than purchase price or standard appraisal value."

"Therefore, the property owner must be sure his policy realistically reflects replacement value, not just purchase price. A thorough appraisal is the starting point," De Negre advises.

54

"It is an excellent precaution to update the appraisal frequently. Construction costs of fine homes are escalating faster than those for average priced homes, and the craftsman able to do detailed work are harder to find."

De Negre suggests that a fine home should be reappraised at least once every seven years, even if no major changes are made, adding that a new appraisal should follow almost any major work, including renovations or additions.

"Remember," he continues, "nobody knows the house as well as the owner. Therefore, it is important for the NEW HOMEOWNER to take the time to go through the entire house with the appraiser and call attention to everything that has been upgraded. An insurable value can then be agreed upon, based upon the appraiser's expertise and the owner's opinion."

De Negre, who is the national manager of CHUBB'S residential appraisers, has compiled a list, based on the collective experience of the company's 100 full-time appraisers of fine homes. He warns to always anticipate increasing costs.

These special items, listed below, are probably applicable to every NEW HOMEOWNER, whether or not you consider your home "upscale."

1. CARPETING: High quality wall-to-wall carpeting will appreciate in value.

2. CRAFTING and FINISHING DETAILS: Duplicating the hand-crafted work or special finishing done by experts can raise the cost immeasureably.

3. EXOTIC FLOORING: Costly wood, marble, imported tile or true parquet flooring will raise replacement costs, though few appraisals take this into account.

4. FIRE EQUIPMENT: Be sure and list a residential fire sprinkler system which was installed before the completion of the house.

5. FIREPLACES: Customizing features such as Art Deco moldings, inlaid marble, Wedgewood facings, carved woodwork or special materials easily raise replacement costs by thousands of dollars.

6. HOME SECURITY EQUIPMENT: If specially installed, this additional cost must also be considered.

7. HOME UTILITIES: Heating and cooling systems represent a sizeable portion of a home's value in the event of a loss. Electric installations for the increasingly popular low-voltage lighting systems far exceed "normal" allowances in insurance appraisals.

8. KITCHEN: Commercial quality equipment raises the cost of replacement.

9. LIGHTING FIXTURES: Custom track lighting, crystal chandeliers, historic sconces should be appraised accordingly. The average 1986 walk-through appraisal would list built-in light fixtures as being worth a standard $250.00 each.

10. OUT-BUILDINGS: a greenhouse equipped with expensive heating, cooling and sprinkler systems, containing orchids or other exotic plants; cabana by the pool; staff facilities; or a well equipped office.

11. PANELING: Value depends not only on type of wood, but labor costs to replace any special crafting such as "fielded," or raised frame panels, hand carving, etc.

55

12. PLUMBING: Quality fixtures in kitchen and multiple bathrooms, for instance, when gold fixtures are used, add a surprisingly high figure to the appraisal.

13. RAILINGS or STAIRCASES: Hand crafting, spiral designs, historic wrought iron, costly woods, special moldings and baseboards all make these items very costly to replace.

14. SOLAR EQUIPMENT: Installation of solar water heaters, which requires additional electrical wiring to accomodate the necessary circulating pumps, etc., adds to the replacement cost of the electrical system.

15. STEREO EQUIPMENT: Special built-in items can raise the replacement cost thousands of dollars.

16. WALLS and WINDOW TREATMENTS: the 1986 standard appraisal for wall coverings and draperies is $1,000 per room; well below replacement costs for padded silk, handpainted fabrics or other special wall coverings and matching custom draperies. Costs can run 10 times more than the standard estimate.

17. WINDOWS: Leaded or stained glass windows are impossible to replace at the formula for common windows.

18. WINE CELLAR: A well stocked, specially equipped wine cellar should not be overlooked, as replacement cost could be enormous.

As a final safeguard, your insurance policy should "schedule," or separately itemize, any above-standard or unique items in your home, along with their replacement value.

"If in doubt, schedule it," DeNegre concludes. "This avoids having to settle for standard replacement benefits if a loss occurs."

STATES REQUIRING LICENSING OF GENERAL CONTRACTORS AND STATE CONSUMER PROTECTION AGENCIES

In an effort to present information about those states that require the licensing of General Contractors, the author has done intensive, comprehensive research in order to make this information available to you. It is shown below together with the list of each state's Consumer Protection Agency.

By definition, a GENERAL Contractor is an individual, firm or corporation who undertakes the building of an entire structure according to its plans and specifications.

In contrast, a sub-contractor is one who enters into a contract with the General Contractor to perform a portion of the work necessary to complete the project. Sub-contractors perform portions of the entire job such as plumbing, electrical, concrete, framing, finish carpentry, roofing, heating & cooling, etc.

The fact that a state may not license General Contractors does not necessarily mean that there are not licensing requirements for either General or sub-contractors on a local (city or county) level.

56

It is interesting to note that some states, even though they require the licensing of General Contractors, do so only to collect additional state revenue! One would think that if they go to the trouble of setting up the licensing process, they would go the rest of the way and require examinations to test the competency and monitor the ethical conduct of their licensees.

After having checked to see if your state requires the licensing of General Contractors, you may then want to investigate if licensing is required at the local level.

LICENSING	CONSUMER PROTECTION
ALABAMA	
License required for any job over $20,000. Executive Secretary, Alabama State Licensing Board for General Contractors 125 So. Ripley St., Montgomery, AL 36130 (205) 261-2839	Consumer Protection Div. Off. of Attorney General 138 Adams Ave. Montgomery, AL 36130 (205)261-4200
ALASKA	
License required. Dept. of Commerce & Economic Development. Division of Occupational Licensing Pouch D, Juneau, AK 99811	Chief, Consumer Protection Section Dept. of Law 1031 W. Fourth Ave. Suite 110 Anchorage, AK 99501 (907) 279-0428

LICENSING	CONSUMER AFFAIRS

ARIZONA

License required.	Financial Fraud Div.
Registrar,	Off. of Attorney General
Arizona State Registrar of	1275 W. Washington
Contractors	#259
1818 West Adams,	Phoenix, AZ 85007
Phoenix, AZ 85007-2671	(602) 255-3702
(602) 255-1525	

ARKANSAS

License required for jobs	Director,
over $20,000.	Consumer Protection Div.
Administrator,	Off. of Attorney General
Arkansas Contractors Licensing	Justice Bldg.
Board,	Little Rock, AR 72201
621 East Capitol Avenue,	(501) 371-2341
Little Rock, AR 72202	
(501) 372-4661	

57

CALIFORNIA

License required on jobs	Director,
over $200.	Dept. of Consumer
Registrar,	Affairs
California Contractors State	1020 N. St., Rm. 516
License Board	Sacramento, CA 95814
P.O. Box 26000,	(916) 445-4465
Sacramento, CA 95827	
(916) 366-5243	

COLORADO

License **not** required.	Director,
	Antitrust/Consumer
	Protection
	Dept. of Law
	1525 Sherman St., 2nd Fl.
	Denver, CO 80203
	(303) 866-3611

CONNECTICUT

License **not** required.	Commissioner,
	Consumer Protection
	Dept.
	165 Capitol Ave.
	Hartford, CT 06106
	(203) 566-4999

LICENSING	CONSUMER PROTECTION

DELAWARE

License required for revenue
only. No examination required.
Department of Finance,
   Division of Revenue
State Office Bldg.
601 Delaware Avenue,
Wilmington, DE 19889

Secretary,
Dept. of Community Affairs
156 S. State St.
Dover, DE 19901
(302) 736-4456

DISTRICT OF COLUMBIA

License **not** required.

Chief,
Off. of Consumer
   Education & Information
Consumer & Regulatory
   Affairs Dept.
614 H St., NW, Rm.108
Washington, DC 20001
(202) 727-7067

58

FLORIDA

License required.
Executive Director,
Florida Construction Industry
   Licensing Board
P.O. Box 2,
Jacksonville, FL 32201
(904) 359-6317

Director,
Div. of Consumer
   Services
Agriculture & Consumer
   Services Dept.
Mayo Bldg.
Tallahassee, FL 32301
(904) 488-2221

GEORGIA

License required.
Executive Director,
Georgia Construction Industry
   Licensing Board,
166 Pryor Street, S.W.,
Atlanta, GA 30303
(404) 656-3939

Administrator,
Off of Consumer Affairs
Off. of Planning &
   Budget
205 Butler St., SE Plaza-E
Atlanta, GA 30334
(404) 656-1760

HAWAII

License required.Director,
Executive Secretary,
Hawaii Contractors Licensing Board,
Professional & Vocational
   Licensing Division
Dept. of Commerce and Consumer Affairs
P.O. Box 3469,
Honolulu, HI 96801
(808) 548-7637

Off of Consumer
   Protection
Commerce & Consumer
   Affairs Dept.
1010 Richards St.
Honolulu, HI 96813
(808) 548-2560

LICENSING	CONSUMER AFFAIRS

IDAHO

Licenses required only for electrical and plumbing.	Attorney General, Off. of Attorney General Statehouse Boise, ID 83720 (208) 334-2400

ILLINOIS

License **not** required.	Attorney General 500 S. Second St. Springfield, IL 62706 (217) 782-1090

INDIANA

License **not** required.	Assistant Director, Div. of Consumer Protection Off. of Attorney General 215 State House Indianapolis, IN 46204 (317) 232-6330

59

IOWA

License **not** required.	Director, Consumer Protection Div. Off. of Attorney General Hoover State Off. Bldg. Des Moines, IA 50319 (515) 281-5926

KANSAS

License **not** required.	Deputy Attorney General, Consumer Protection Div. Off. of Attorney General Judicial Ctr. Topeka, KS 66612 (913) 296-3751

KENTUCKY

License **not** required.	Attorney General State Capitol Frankfort, KY 40601 (502) 564-7600

LICENSING	CONSUMER AFFAIRS
	LOUISIANA
License required on work over $50,000. Executive Director, Louisiana State Licensing Board for Contractors 7434 Perkins Road, Baton Rouge, LA 70808 (504) 766-9751	Assistant Secretary, Off. of Consumer Protection Urban & Community Affairs Dept. P.O. Box 94455 Baton Rouge, LA 70804-9455 (504) 925-4410
	MAINE
License **not** required.	Superintendent, Bur. of Consumer Credit Protection Business, Occupational & Professional Regulations Dept. State House Station #35 Augusta, ME 04333 (207) 289-3731
	MARYLAND
License required. Maryland State Licensing Board for Contractors State License Bureau 301 W. Preston Street, Room 404, Baltimore, MD 21201	Chief, Consumer & Investor Affairs Div. Off. of Attorney General 7 N. Calvert St. Baltimore, MD 21202 (301) 576-6550
	MASSACHUSETTS
License **not** required.	Secretary, Exec. Off. of Consumer Affairs One Ashburton Pl. Boston, MA 02108 (617) 727-7755
	MICHIGAN
License required. Director of Licensing, Michigan Department of Licensing and Regulation P.O. Box 30018, Lansing, MI 48909 (517) 373-0505	Director, Regulatory & Consumer Affairs Dept. of Commerce P.O. Box 30221 Lansing, MI 48909 (517) 373-8681

60

LICENSING	CONSUMER PROTECTION

MINNESOTA

License **not** required.	Special Assistant Attorney General, Consumer Div. Off. of Attorney General 117 University Ave. St. Paul, MN 55155 (612) 296-2306

MISSISSIPPI

License **not** required.	Assistant Attorney General, Consumer Protection Div. Off. of Attorney General 5th Fl., Gartin Bldg. Jackson, MS 39201 (601) 359-3095

MISSOURI

License **not** required.	Director, Dept. of Economic Development Truman Bldg. P.O. Box 1157 Jefferson City, MO 65102 (314) 751-4962

MONTANA

License required. Montana Dept. of Revenue. Miscellaneous Tax Division, Mitchell Building, Helena, MT 59601	Attorney/Unit Manager, Consumer Affairs Unit Dept. of Commerce 1424 Ninth Ave. Helena, MT 59620 (406) 444-4313

NEBRASKA

License required. Nebraska State Home Builders Assoc, 1115 K Street, Lincoln, NE 68508	Consumer Fraud Section, Off. of Attorney General P.O. Box 94906 Lincoln, NE 68509-4906 (402) 471-2682

LICENSING	CONSUMER PROTECTION

NEVADA

License required.
Executive Officer,
Nevada State Contractors Board
1800 Industrial Road,
Las Vegas, NV 89102
(702) 385-0101

Commissioner,
Div. of Consumer Affairs
Dept. of Commerce
2501 E. Sahara Ave., #202
Las Vegas, NV 89518
(702) 386-5293

NEW HAMPSHIRE

License **not** required.

Attorney General,
208 State House Annex
235 Capitol St.
Concord, NH 03301-6397
(603) 271-3658

NEW JERSEY

62

License **not** required,

Director,
Div. of Consumer Affairs
Dept. of Law & Public
  Safety
1100 Raymond Blvd.
Rm. 504
Newark, NJ 07102
(201) 648-4010

NEW MEXICO

License required.
New Mexico Construction
  Industries Division
Bataan Memorial Bldg,
Santa Fe, NM 87503-9990
(505) 827-6260

Director,
Consumer Protection &
Economic Crimes Div.
Off. of Attorney General
Bataan Memorial Bldg.
Santa Fe, NM 87503
(505) 827-6060

NEW YORK

License **not** required.

Director,
Consumer Protection Bd.
Twin Towers
99 Washington Ave.
Albany, NY 12210
(518) 474-3514

LICENSING	CONSUMER PROTECTION
NORTH CAROLINA	
License required. Director, North Carolina State Licensing Board 　for General Contractors P.O. Box 17187, Raleigh, NC 27619 (919) 733-9325	Deputy Attorney General, Consumer Protection Div. Dept. of Justice Justice Bldg., Box 629 Raleigh, NC 27602 (919) 733-7741
NORTH DAKOTA	
License required. Secretary of State, State Capitol Bismarck, ND 58505	Attorney, Consumer Fraud Div. Off. of Attorney General 17th Fl., State Capitol Bismarck, ND 58505 (701) 224-3404
OHIO	
• License **not** required.	Consumers Counsel, Off. of Consumers 　Counsel 137 E. State St. Columbus, OH 43215 (614) 466-9545
OKLAHOMA	
License **not** required.	Administrator, Consumer Credit Dept. 2101 N. Lincoln Blvd. Oklahoma City, OK 73105 (405) 521-3653
OREGON	
License required. Department of Commerce, Builders Board, Salem, OR 97310	Chief Counsel, Div. of Consumer 　Protection & Services Dept. of Justice 520 SW Yamhill Portland, OR 97204 (503) 229-5548
PENNSYLVANIA	
License **not** required.	Director, Bur. of Consumer 　Protection Off. of Attorney General Strawberry Sq., 14th Fl. Harrisburg, PA 17120 (717) 787-9707

63

LICENSING	CONSUMER PROTECTION

RHODE ISLAND

License **not** required.

Executive Director,
Consumers' Council
365 Broadway
Providence, RI 02902
(401) 277-2764

SOUTH CAROLINA

License required.
Executive Director,
South Carolina State Licensing
  Board for Contractors
P.O. Box 5737
Columbia, SC 29250
(803) 758-2355

Administrator,
Dept. of Consumer
  Affairs
2221 Devine St.
P.O. Box 5757
Columbia, SC 29250-5757
(803) 758-3017

64

SOUTH DAKOTA

License **not** required.

Assistant Attorney
  General,
Div. of Consumer Affairs
Off. of Attorney General
State Capitol
Pierre, SD 57501
(605) 773-4400

TENNESSEE

License required for work
  in excess of $50,000.
Executive Director,
Tennessee Board for Licensing
  General Contractors
Doctors Building, Suite 522,
706 Church Street,
Nashville, TN 37219
(615) 741-7984

Director,
Div. of Consumer Affairs
Dept. of Commerce
  & Insurance
206 State Office Bldg.
Nashville, TN 37219
(615) 741-4737

TEXAS

License **not** required.

Director,
Div. of Consumer Affairs
Off. of Attorney General
P.O. Box 12548
Austin, TX 78711
(512) 475-2060

LICENSING

CONSUMER PROTECTION

UTAH

License required.
Administrator,
Utah Dept. of Business
  Regulation,
Department of Contractors,
P.O. Box 5802,
Salt Lake City, UT 84110
(801) 530-6742

Administrative Secretary,
Consumer Services Cmte.
Dept. of Business
  Regulation
160 E. 300 S.
Salt Lake City, UT 84110-5802
(801) 530-6645

VERMONT

License **not** required.

Chief,
Public Protection Div.
Off. of Attorney General
109 State St.
Montpelier, VT 05602
(802) 828-3171

65

VIRGINIA

License required.
Executive Director,
Virginia State Registration
  Board for Contractors
Department of Commerce
3600 West Broad Street,
Richmond, VA 23230

Director,
Consumer Affairs Off.
Agriculture & Consumer
  Services Dept.
1100 Bank St.
Richmand, VA 23219
(804) 786-2042

WASHINGTON

License required.
Assistant Director,
Washington Dept. of Labor
  and Industries,
Dept. of Labor and
  Industries
Building and Construction
  Safety Inspection
  Services Division,
520 South Water Street,
Olympia, WA 98504
(206) 754-1585

Chief,
Off. of Consumer Protection
Off. of Attorney General
Dexter Horton Bldg.
Seattle, WA 98104
(206) 464-6446

LICENSING	CONSUMER PROTECTION
	WEST VIRGINIA
License **not** required.	Dep. Attorney General, Consumer Protection Div. Off. of the Atty. General 3412 Staunton Ave. SE Charleston, WV 25304 (304) 348-8986
	WISCONSIN
License **not** required.	Dept. of Ag., Trade & Consumer Protection P.O. Box 8911 Madison, WI 53708 (608) 266-7100
	WYOMING
License **not** required.	Attorney General, State Capitol Cheyenne, WY 82002 (307) 777-7841

66

GLOSSARY

A

ACOUSTICAL TILE: Special tile for walls and ceilings made of mineral, wood, vegetable fibers, cork or metal. Its purpose is to control sound volume, while providing cover. Most often used in remodeling older dwellings to hide or lower height of old ceilings and in commercial work.

AIR DUCT: Pipes that carry warm air and cold air to rooms and back to furnace or air conditioning system.

APRON: A paved area, such as the juncture of a driveway with the street or with a gargage entrance.

AWNING: A roof-like shelter extending over a doorway, window, porch, etc., which provides protection from the sun or rain.

AWNING WINDOW: A window in which the vent or vents pivot outward from the top edge, giving an awning effect.

B

BALUSTERS: Upright supports of a balustrade rail.

BALUSTRADE: A row of balusters topped by a rail, edging a balcony or a staircase.

BASEBOARD: A horizontal molding used to cover the joint between a wall and floor.

BASE SHOE MOLDING: Molding used next to the floor on baseboard. Usually used on vinyl or wood floors.

BATT: Insulation in the form of a blanket, rather than loose filling.

BATTEN: A narrow strip of wood or metal used to cover vertical joints between boards or panels. See Board and Batten.

BEAM: The main horizontal members of a building installed so as to support the load of the structure. They may be made of wood, metal or other materials.

BEAM CEILING: A type of construction in which the supporting beams of the ceiling are exposed to view.

BEARING WALL: A wall that supports a floor or roof of a building.

BELOW GRADE: An area which is located below the ground level.

BEVEL SIDING: Finish siding for the exterior of a building. It is cut so that it is wedge-shaped and is installed with the thicker edge at the bottom so as to give a "shadow" effect to the finished wall. See Clapboard.

68

BIB OR BIBCOCK:	A water faucet to which a hose may be attached also called a hose bib or sill cock.
BIRD SCREEN:	Wire mesh used to prevent birds or rodents from entering the building through louvers or ventilators.
BLACKTOP:	A general term referring to asphalt paving.
BOARD AND BATTEN:	A type of vertical siding constructed of wide boards and narrow battens. The boards are usually about 12 inches wide and the battens, usually about two or three inches wide, are nailed over the joints of the boards.
BRACE:	A piece of wood or other material used to form a triangle and stiffen some part of a structure.
BREEZEWAY:	A covered passage way between the house and garage.
BRICK VENEER:	Brick used as the decorative outer surface of a framed wall.
BUILT-UP ROOF:	A roofing material applied in sealed, water-proof layers, where there is only a slight slope to the roof.
BUTT JOINT:	Joining point of two pieces of wood or molding with the ends meeting but not overlapping.

69

C

CANTILEVER:	A beam, projecting from a wall and supported at only one end, which is used to support something such as a balcony.
CASEMENT WINDOW:	A window sash that opens on hinges at the vertical edge.

CASING: The framework around a door or window.

CAULKING: The process of filling and sealing joints to prevent the penetration of moisture.

CHAIR RAIL: Wood molding on a wall around a room at the level of of a chair back.

CHASE: A groove or tunnel through a wall or floor to accommodate pipes, ducts or wires.

CHIMNEY CAP: Concrete capping around the top of the chimney bricks to protect the masonry from the elements.

CIRCUIT BREAKER: A safety device which opens(breaks) an electric circuit automatically when it becomes overloaded.

CLAP-BOARD: A board that is thin on one edge and thicker on the other which is installed overlapped to form a weatherproof, exterior wall surface.

CORBEL: A horizontal projection from a wall, forming a ledge or supporting a structure above it.

CORNER BEAD: A strip of wood or metal for protecting the external corners of plastered walls.

CORNICE: A projection at the top of the wall, under the eaves, or where the roof and side walls meet.

COURSE: A horizontal row of bricks, cinder blocks or other masonry materials.

COVE: A concave (a curved recess, hollowed out like the inner curve of a circle) molding applied at the point where a wall meets the ceiling.

70

COVE LIGHTING: Concealed light sources behind a cornice or horizontal recess which direct the light upon a relecting ceiling.

CRAWL SPACE: A shallow, unfinished space beneath the first floor of a house which has no basement, used for visual inspection and access to pipes and ducts. Also, a shallow space in the attic, immediately under the roof.

CRIPPLES: Short framing studs above and below windows.

D

DAMPER: A mechanical device used for regulating the flow of air up a chimney.

DEAD BOLT: A locking bolt that has no spring and must be activated by using a key or thumb latch. Usually installed on exterior doors.

DISTRIBUTION BOX: Also called a meter box. A box into which the main electrical feed enters and is then distributed to the individual circuits.

DOORJAMB: The case which surrounds a door into which it opens and closes.

DOORSILL: A horizontal specially shaped piece of wood or metal installed at the base of the frame on an outside door. Also known as a threshold, it is fastened to the floor designed to keep out the the rain and drafts.

DOOR STOP: A device used to hold a door open at any desired position. The term is also used to describe the strip of wood or metal against which a door closes.

71

DORMER:	A projection built out from a sloping roof usually having a window on its front surface.
DOUBLE GLAZING:	Two sheets of glass bonded together at the edges with an air space in between. Provides insulation against the passage of heat or cold.
DOUBLE HUNG WINDOWS:	Windows with an upper and lower sash, each supported by cords or weights.
DOWNSPOUT:	A spout or pipe to carry rain water down from a roof or gutters.
DRIP CAP:	A molding placed above the outside of a door indow which causes the water to drip either to the sides or beyond the outside of the frame.
DRYWALL CONSTRUCTION:	A wall surface of plasterboard, sheetrock or material other than plaster.
DUCT:	In a house, round or square metal pipe, made of ious materials, used for distributing heated air from the heating plant to rooms or cool air from an air conditioning system.
DUPLEX OUTLET:	An electrical wall outlet having two plug receptacles.

72

E

EAVES:	That part of a roof which projects out beyond the side walls.
ELL:	An extension or wing of a building at right angles to the main section. Also. a pipe shaped as a bent elbow or L.
ESCUTCHEON:	A shield or decorative plate for door hardware, plumbing fixtures, etc.

F

FASCIA: A flat horizontal board attached to the ends of the projecting roof beams.

FILL-TYPE INSULATION: Loose insulating material which is applied by hand or blown into wall spaces mechanically.

FLASHING: Noncorrosive sheet metal, such as galvanized steel, aluminum, copper, lead or tin, used around angles or junctions in roofs and exterior walls to prevent leaks.

FLAT PAINT: A type of paint that contains a high proportion of pigment and dries to a flat or lusterless finish.

FLAT ROOF: A roof with no peaks or valleys having only sufficient slope for drainage.

FLAT SKYLIGHT: Any skylight which has only enough pitch to carry off rain water or water from melting snow.

FLEX-DUCT: A flexible rounded duct, made of spiral wire covered with plastic or heavy cloth for use in transfer of air in heating, cooling and ventilating systems and available in various diameters.

FLEXIBLE METAL CONDUIT: Electrical conduit of spirally wound steel strip.

FLOOR BEAM: A transverse beam or girder placed at the panel points of a span to support the stringers that carry the floor.

FLOOR DRAIN: A plumbing fixture used to drain water from floors into the plumbing system. Such drains are usually located in the laundry and in stall showers.

73

FLOOR JOISTS: Framing pieces which rest on outer foundation walls and interior beams or girders.

FLOORING TILES: Concrete or clay tiles set in cement mortar or other adhesive. For a more sound-absorbent heat-insulating, decorative or comfortable walking surface, vinyl, cork, rubber, asphalt or plastic tiles are used.

FLUE: An enclosed passageway, such as a pipe or chimney, for carrying off smoke, gases or fumes to the outside air.

FLUE LINING: The tile or pipe inside a chimney.

FLUSH DOOR: A door any size, not paneled, having two flat surfaces; flush doors are frequently of various types of hollow core construction.

FLUSH TANK: The reservoir from which a toilet is flushed with water.

FOOTING: Concrete base on which is positioned the wall of a house.

FORCED AIR: Hot or cold air blown from a heating or air-conditioning unit by means of a fan or blower.

FORCED AIR FURNACE: A heating unit fitted with a fan or blower to circulate the heated air.

FORMICA: The trade name for a hard, laminated plastic sheeting used for table, sink and counter tops or for wall or cabinet door covering. It is extremely resistant to damage.

FOUNDATION: The entire masonry substructure below the first floor or frame of a building, including the footing upon which the building rests; also the soil or rock upon which a building or other structure rests.

74

FRAME
CONSTRUCTION: The building of houses, apartments, etc, using wood framing lumber.

FRAMING: The frame or skeleton of the house including the beams, studs and rafters.

FRENCH
WINDOW: A doorway equipped with two glazed doors hinged at the jambs.

FULL GLOSS: A painting term for the highest possible grade of gloss.

FUSE: A replaceable fusible link in the wiring for an electric circuit to break the circuit by melting in the event of an overload.

FUSE BOX: A term sometimes applied to a distribution fuse board when it is enclosed in a box.

75

G

GABLE: The triangular part of a wall under the inverted "V" of the roof line.

GALVANIZED
IRON: Steel or sheet steel (usually not iron), coated with zinc.

GALVANIZED
PIPE: Zinc coated pipe for water flow. Gas pipe is black.

GAMBREL ROOF: A roof with two pitches, designed to provide more space on upper floors. The roof is steeper on its lower slope and flatter toward the ridge.

GAS MAIN: The community pipe line that supplies gas to individual units for heating, air conditioning and cooking.

GAS METER: A measuring and recording device for gas used in your home.

GIRDER: A main beam in a framed floor supporting the joists which carry the flooring boards. It carries the weight of a floor or partition.

GLAZING: Fitting the glass into windows or doors.

GRADE: The slope of a road, channel or natural ground.

GRADING: Modification of the ground surface by cuts, fills or both.

GRADE LINE: The point at which the ground rests against the foundation wall.

GROUND LINE: In building construction, the ground level or natural grade line from which measurements for excavating are taken.

GROUT: A mixture of cement, sand, and water, or cement and water, made so thin that it will run into joints and cavities of masonry; also the hardened equivalent of such mixture.

GROUT JOINT: An even spacing between tiles that is filled with grout.

GUTTER: A shallow channel or conduit of metal or wood set below and along the eaves of a house to catch and carry off rain water.

GYPSUM WALLBOARD: A prefabricated sheet used in drywall construction as a substitute for plaster; made of gypsum covered with paper which can be painted, textured or wall papered.

H

HALLWAY: A corridor; an entry.

HANDRAIL: A bar or pipe supported on brackets from a wall or partition, as on a stairway or ramp, to provide a handhold.

HEADERS: Double wood pieces supporting joists in a floor or double wood studs placed on edge over windows and doors to transfer the roof and floor weight to the studs.

HEADER JOIST: In carpentry, the large beam or timber into which the common joists are fitted when framing around openings for stairs, chimneys or any opening in a floor or roof. It is placed between two long beams and supports the ends of short timbers.

HEARTH: The floor of a fireplace. Also the portion of the floor immediately in front of the fireplace, usually made of brick, tile or stone.

77

HEATING SYSTEM, HOT WATER: A system of heating, utilizing hot water circulated through pipes, coils and radiators.

HEATING SYSTEM, STEAM: A steam heating system employing steam at pressures between 0 and 15 pounds pressure.

HEATING SYSTEM, WARM AIR: A warm air heating plant, consisting of a heating unit(fuel-burning furnace) enclosed in a casing, from which the heated air is distributed through ducts to various rooms of the house.

HIP: The external angle formed by the juncture of two slopes of a roof.

HIP ROOF: A roof that slants upward on three or four sides.

HOLIDAY: A painter's term for a skip in the application of material or paint.

HOLLOW-CORE DOOR: A flush door in which plywood or hard wood for both sides is glued to a skeleton framework. It is lighter and less expensive than a solid door.

HOOD: Overhead cover of a chimney or a kitchen range; also an inverted funnel leading into a ventilating flue.

HOT-AIR HEATER: A system of heating by driving warm air into a room through vents in the walls or floor.

HUMID-IFICATION: The process of adding moisture to heated air by means of evaporation.

HUMIDIFIER: A mechanical device which controls the amount of water vapor to be added to the atmosphere.

78

I

INDIRECT HEATING: Heating of rooms by a distant source of heat which is brought to each room by steam, water or hot air; also known as Central Heating.

INDIRECT LIGHTING: A system of artifical lighting in which light from the sources is directed at ceiling or wall to be reflected for general illumination.

INDOOR/ OUTDOOR: Type of carpet, regardless of construction, which is made entirely of components(surface yarns, backing, adhesives or laminating materials) which have been especially designed or treated to withstand moisture, extremes of temperature, ultraviolet rays and other types of exposure.

INSULATION: Any material used in building construction for the reduction of fire hazard or for protection from heat or cold.

J

JALOUSIE WINDOW: A window made of horizontal adjustable sections or louvers that control ventilation.

JAMB: An upright surface that outlines an opening for a door or window.

JOINT: In carpentry, the place where two or more surfaces meet; also, to form or unite, two pieces so that they will fit together properly when joined.

JOIST: A heavy piece of horizontal timber to which the boards of a floor, or the lath of a ceiling are nailed. Joists, laid edgewise to form the floor support, rest on the wall or on girders.

JOIST HANGER: A steel or iron stirrup used to support and align the ends of joists which are to be fastened to the girder.

79

L

LALLY COLUMN: Trade name for a cylindrically-shaped steel column, sometimes filled with concrete, used as a support for girders or other beams.

LAMINATED PLASTIC: Sheets of paper or textile, soaked with a synthetic resin, sandwiched between layers of the resin to make a rigid sheet with glossy-surfaced covering; Formica, for example.

LANDING: A platform in a flight of stairs between two stories; also the terminating or the changing of a stairway.

LATEX PAINTS: Water-base paints, sometimes called "vinyl" or "acrylic" paints; cleanup and thinning are done with water.

LINTEL: The top framing beam over a door or window which supports the wall above the opening.

LOAD-BEARING WALL: A strong wall capable of supporting its own weight as well as other weight and force of wind. Same as a supporting wall. (Partitions and panel walls are usually not load bearing.)

LOUVER: An opening with horizontal slats to permit the ventilation of closed attics, closets or other storage areas and spaces.

M

80

MACADAM: A commonly used method of paving with crushed stone, named for John L. Macadam(1756-1836), a Scottish engineer. The road may be water-bound, cement-bound, or coated with asphalt or tar.

MAIN BEAM: In floor construction, one of the principal beams which transmits loads directly to the columns, not onto another beam.

MANSARD ROOF: A roof with two slopes or pitches on each of the four sides, the lower slopes steeper than the upper.

MASONRY: Walls, fireplaces, chimneys and foundations constructed of brick, stone, tile or similar materials.

METAL VALLEY: A valley type roof joint lined with metal such as lead, copper, zinc or galvanized steel.

MOISTURE BARRIER: Treated paper, metal or plastic that retards or prevents moisture from seeping into walls or floors.

MOLDING: A strip of decorative material having a plane or curved narrow surface and used for ornamental application. These strips are often used to hide gaps at wall junctures.

MUD: Slang: concrete or mortar; drywall taping compound.

MULLION: The thin vertical bars which divide the lights or panes in a windows or the panels in a door.

N

NAIL: A slender piece of metal pointed at one end for driving into wood as a fastener. It is flat or rounded at the other end for striking with a hammer. The size of nails is described by the term "penny," abbreviated "d" which originally indicated the price per hundred, but now refers to the length. Although the sizes of nails may vary as much as $1/8$ to $1/4$ inch from that indicated, the approximate lengths sold are: 4 penny nail = $1\frac{1}{4}$ inches; 6 penny = 2 inches; 8 penny = $2\frac{1}{2}$ inches; 10 penny = 3 inches; 20 penny = 4 inches; 60 penny = 6 inches, etc.

81

NAIL POP: An abnormal flaw, where the fastener has moved outward relative to the board, usually because of improper wallboard application or lumber shrinkage.

NEWEL POST: The upright post supporting the handrail at the top and bottom of a stairway or at a landing; also the main post about which a circular staircase winds; a stone column carrying the inner ends of the treads of a spiral stone staircase.

NEWEL CAP:	A top or cap for the newel post.
NOSING:	The rounded half-round, overhanging edge of a stair tread, flat roof, window sill, etc.

O

ORANGE PEEL:	Term used to describe: poorly applied paint resulting in a pocked effect and resembling the peel of an orange; pinholing; a texture design applied to walls in drywalling.
OUTLET:	A distribution source of electrical current, such as for a lighting fixture, or a socket into which can be plugged lamps or other electrical appliances.
OUT-OF-PLUMB:	A term used when referring to a structural column which is not in alignment; not truly vertical or leaning away from the vertical.
OVERHEAD DOOR:	A counterbalanced door, used in garages, that opens by following side tracks to a horizontal position above and behind the opening. May be in one or more leaves.

82

P

PANE:	A sheet of glass fitted into the opening in a window sash or door.
PANEL BOX:	A box in which electric switches and fuses for branch circuits are located.
PANEL HEATING:	A method of home heating by means of electric or hot water coils installed in ceilings, walls, floors or baseboards.

PARQUET FLOOR:	A hardwood floor laid in small rectangular or square patterns, not in long strips, to form various designs.
PARTITION:	A dividing wall between rooms or areas, generally non-bearing.
PARTY WALL:	A wall erected on a line between adjoining properties and used in common. This can be either an interior or exterior wall.
PAVING:	Generally a layer of concrete, asphalt or coated macadam. Used on streets, sidewalks and pathways.
PEAK:	The uppermost point of a gable.
PEAKED ROOF:	A roof rising either to a point or a ridge.
PERIMETER HEATING:	A method of warm air heating whereby the hot air registers are installed near outside walls beneath windows.
PICKET:	One of the upright wooden stakes supported by upper and lower rails between posts in a type of fence.
PILOT LIGHT:	A small flame, used in gas-heating devices, which burns constantly.
PITCH:	The angle of slope of a roof.
PLASTER:	A cementitious material or combination of cementitious material and aggregate that, when mixed with a suitable amount of water, forms a plastic mass or paste which, when applied to a surface, adheres to it and subsequently hardens, preserving in a rigid state the form or texture imposed during the period of plasticity; also the placed and hardened mixture.
PLASTERBOARD:	Gypsum board, used instead of plaster.

PLENUM: An air compartment connected to one or more inlets or outlets.

PLUMB: True according to a plumb line; perpendicular; vertical; to true up vertically as a wall by use of a plumb line.

PLYWOOD: A fabricated wood product constructed of three or more layers of veneer joined with glue, usually laid with grain of adjoining plies at right angles.

PORCH: A roofed structure providing shelter at the entrance of a building; an open or enclosed room on the outside of a building.

PRIMER: The first coat in a series of applications of two or more coats of paint.

PUNCH LIST: A list, made by the builder near the completion of work listing items still to be furnished or work to be performed by the sub-contractors in order to complete the house as specified in the contract documents. (Author's note: If this list is made up carefully, you should not find too many things wrong when you do your walk-through.)

PUTTY: A stiff, doughlike material consisting of pigment and vehicle, used for setting window panes and filling imperfections in wood or metal surfaces.

Q

QUARRY TILE: In masonry, a name given to machine-made, unglazed tile; also called promenade tile.

QUARTER-ROUND: Molding strips presenting the profile of a quarter circle.

84

R

RADIANT HEATING:	A method of heating, consisting of coils of electrically heated wires, or heated water pipes, embedded in the floor, wall or ceiling of a room.
RADIATOR,	The room heating unit of a hot water or steam heating system.
RAFTER:	One of a series of structural roof beams, spanning from an exterior wall to a center ridge beam or ridge board, designed to support roof loads. The rafters of a flat roof are sometimes called roof joists.
RANDOM WIDTHS:	The term used in describing flooring and wall boards or shingles of varying widths.
READY-MIXED CONCRETE:	Concrete manufactured for delivery to this building site in a wet, unhardened state.
REDWOOD:	A tree indigenous to California, whose lightweight, reddish wood is decay resistant, used in building for both exterior and interior work, and for structural timber.
REGISTER:	The end of a duct for incoming or escaping air which is usually covered with grillework.
REINFORCED CONCRETE:	Concrete strengthened with wire or metal bars.
RETURN AIR DUCT:	Ducts through which the cold air or return air passes on its way back to the heating unit.
RIDGE:	The top horizontal edge or peak of a roof.
RIDGE POLE:	A thick longitudinal plank to which the ridge rafters of a roof are attached.

85

RISER:	The upright piece or vertical board of a stair step, from tread to tread in a staircase.
ROLL ROOFING:	A roofing material, supplied in rolls, and made of compressed fibers saturated with asphalt.
ROOF OVERHANG:	A roof extension beyond the endwall or sidewall of a building.
ROOF SHEATHING:	Sheets, usually of plywood, which are nailed to the top edges of trusses or rafters to tie the roof together and support the roofing material.
ROUGH FLOOR:	Rough floor boards on which the finished floor is laid. In quality work, a layer of building paper separates these two floors.
ROUGHING IN:	The installation of all concealed plumbing electrical, heating and cooling pipes or wires before the drywall or other finished wall covering is installed over the studs.
"R" VALUE:	In insulation, a measurement of the resistance to heat flow. The higher the "R" value, the more effective the insulation.

86

S

SASH:	The part of the window into which the panes of glass are installed.
SASH AND FRAME:	A cased frame and a sash window comprising the entire window unit.
SASH BALANCE:	A spring operated device which counterbalances the weight of the window sash in double hung window units. These balances eliminate the need need for sash weights, pulleys and cords.

SAW HORSE: A four-legged bench made primarily for use while hand sawing. The legs are usually an inverted V with the top a 2x4 or 2x6 inch piece of lumber.

SCUTTLE HOLE: A small access opening either to the attic or basement crawl space.

SEPTIC TANK: A sewage settling tank in which part of the sewage is converted into gas and sludge before the remaining waste is discharged by gravity into a leaching bed underground. This system is used only when a public sewer system is not available.

SHAKES: A hand-split cedar shingle widely used in the western United States.

SHEATHING: The first layer of exterior wall covering nailed to the studs on an outside wall or roof prior to installing the finished siding or roof covering.

SHEATHING PAPER: Water-resistant paper applied between the sheathing and the outer finished siding or shingles.

SHINGLES: Wood, asbestos, asphalt, slate or other material, cut into stock lengths, widths and thickness, used as an overlapping outer covering on walls or roofs.

SHIPLAP: A type of lumber having a portion of the width cut away on both edges, but on opposite sides, so as to make a flush joint with similar pieces.

SHOE MOLD: The small molding covering the joint between the flooring and the baseboard on the inside of a room.

SIDING: Boards of special design nailed horizontally to the vertical studs to form the exposed surface of the outside walls of a frame house.

SILL: A horizontal closure at the bottom of a door frame. (see threshold)

87

SILL COCK: A faucet or hose connection, usually on the exterior of a building about sill height. Also called hosebib.

SINGLE-POLE SWITCH: An electrical switching device for making or breaking one side of an electric current.

SKYLIGHT: An opening in a roof or ceiling for admitting daylight; also the window fitted into such an opening.

SLAB: Concrete floor or platform poured directly on an earth, gravel or sand base.

SOFFIT: The underside of any subordinate part of a building, such as the under surface of an arch cornice or stairway.

88

SOLAR COLLECTOR: Device (normally constructed of glass, plastic or metal, which extracts heat from the sun and transfers it to fluid or air.

SOLAR ENERGY: The heat energy derived from the sun's rays is commonly referred to as solar energy. Solar energy is used more in the "sun belt" states for house and water heating.

SOLARIUM: A room, the walls and sometimes roof of which are glazed to admit an abundance of sunlight.

SPARK ARRESTER: A screen over the top of a chimney to keep embers from falling to the roof.

STEEL CASEMENT: A window frame and sash made of steel oraluminum in which the window sections swing outward vertically from the side frames.

STORM DOOR: An additional outside door set in the door frame to provide better insulation against the weather.

STORM WINDOW: An additional outside window set in the window frame to provide better insulation against the weather.

STRINGER: A horizontal structural timber supporting joists and resting on vertical supports.

STUCCO: A mortar material applied in a soft state and when dry forms a hard covering for the outside walls or other exterior surfaces on any structure.

STUDS: In wall framing, a series of slender wood timbers to which horizontal pieces are nailed, and used to support elements in walls and partitions. Wall studs are usually spaced 16 inches on center. On center means from the center of one to the center of the next one.

SUB-FLOOR: Usually plywood sheets that are nailed directly to the floor joists and to which the finished floor is later fastened.

SWALE: A wide shallow depression in the ground to form a channel for water drainage.

89

T

TERRAZZO FLOORING: A term used in the building trades for a type of flooring made of small fragments of colored stone or marble embedded irregularly in cement. The surface is then ground to a high polish.

THREE-WAY SWITCH: A switch used in wiring when a light, or lights, is to be turned on or off from two places. A three-way switch must be used at each place.

TONGUE-AND-GROOVE: Sheeting, usually wood, in which one side edge of the board is cut with a projecting tongue that fits into a corresponding groove or recess cut in the opposite edge of an adjoining board.

TRANSOM: An opening over a door or window, usually for ventilation, containing a glazed or solid sash, usually hinged or pivoted.

TRAP: A bend in the water pipe that holds water so sewer gases will not escape into the house.

TREAD: The horizontal part of a stair step.

U

UNDER-LAYMENT: Installed to cover sub-floor irregularities and to absorb the movement of wood subfloors prior to the installation of the finish flooring materials.

V

VALLEY: In architecture, the term applies to a depressed angle formed by the meeting at the bottom of two inclined slopes of a roof.

VAPOR BARRIER: Material such as paper, metal, plastic or paint used to prevent vapor or moisture from passing through a wall, floor or partition into an adjoining area.

VENT PIPE: A flue or pipe connecting any interior space in a house with the outer air for purposes of ventilation; also any small pipe extending from any of the various plumbing fixtures in the house to the vent stack.

VENT STACK: A vertical pipe connected with all vent pipes carrying off foul air or gases from the house. It extends through the roof and provides an outlet for gases and contaminated air.

W

WAINSCOTING: The lower three or four feet of an interior wall of a room when lined with paneling, tile or other material different from the rest of the wall.

WALL SHEATHING: Sheets of plywood, gypsum board or other material nailed to the outside face of studs as a base for exterior siding.

WARM AIR HEATING SYSTEM: A heating system in which furnace-heating air moves to living space through a single register or a series of ducts, circulated by natural convection(gravity system) or by a fan or blower in the duct-work (forced system).

WATER METER: A device for recording the amount of water flowing through a pipe.

WEATHER STRIPPING: Metal, wood, plastic or other material installed around door and window openings to prevent air infiltration.

WEEP HOLE: A small hole in retaining walls, foundations, etc, which permits drainage and reduces pressure against the structure.

Z

ZINC: A metallic element used for galvanizing sheet metal.

ZONING: Restrictions as to the size or character of buildings permitted within specific government jurisdictions. Also restricts the use of land for specific purposes.

PART II

WORKBOOK SECTION

On the following page is a copy of a one year warranty that was used by a California builder. The next page will give you an idea of the types of defects found during an actual walk-through.

Next, you will find work sheets that have been perforated for easy removal. You should make several photocopies of them to use during your practice runs. Save the originals for your actual walk-through.

I suggest practicing first where you live now. Go through room by room and see what you can find wrong. You might be surprised at what you find that you never saw before! This will give you practice in knowing what to write on your list.

You might practice on housing developments being built near you. The more times you do this, the more proficient you will be when the time comes for you to do the walk-through on your own house.

Contained in this book are individual walk-through check list sheets for each room and exterior area. You will probably find them to be more comprehensive than your builder's sheets. I suggest that you use them during your walk-through.

Remember, when doing the walk-through with the builder on your house, don't allow yourself to be rushed through. Take your time and make sure you see everything.

Limited One-Year Warranty

Builder warrants that your new home is free of defective materials and defective construction. We will correct any defect reported within one year from the date of first occupancy or close of escrow, whichever is earlier. This warranty will not make us liable for other injuries or losses, such as bodily injury or property damage occurring to any person or property because of any defect in the house. Some states do not allow the exclusion or limitation of incidental or consequential damages so the above limitation or exclusion may not apply to you. We will determine the materials and methods to be used in making any repair.

This warranty is available only to our home purchaser, and not to any subsequent purchaser. This warranty gives you specific legal rights, and you may also have other rights which vary from state to state.

This warranty does not apply to the following appliances and equipment, which are warranted by the manufacturer. For service to these components, you should call the manufacturer:

- Plumbing
- Electrical
- Water Heater
- Furnace
- Dishwasher, Garbage Disposal and Trash Compactor
- Range, Oven and Hood Fan
- Heating/Air Conditioning Equipment and Controls
- Smoke or Fire Alarm

We will not be responsible for plant materials, hairline cracks in plaster or stucco, leaking faucets, loose or broken towel bars or soap dishes, broken or damaged floor tiles, or concrete cracks except for cracks of such magnitude as to substantially interrupt the plane of the surface or affect its structural integrity. We will not be responsible for the repair of appliances or services which are damaged by unreasonable or unauthorized use, or for damage caused by lack of normal and proper homeowner maintenance. We will not be responsible for leakage of the roof due to the installation of any appliance or television antenna. We will not be responsible for damage caused by improper landscaping or watering, or changing the grade of your yard.

For warranty service, you must notify us in writing at
        This warranty is a legal obligation, and may be enforced as such in the unlikely event that you believe we have not lived up to our obligations.

_____   _____

WALK THROUGH INSPECTION REPORT

FOR: *John & Jane Doe*
(Buyer's Name)
AGREEMENT OF ACCEPTANCE

    I/We hereby declare that, in the company of an accredited representative of Seller, I/We have received the keys and have inspected the residential property known as LOT *38* TRACT *175*, located at *1234 Main Street, Sunny*, California, and that I/We accept the property as being constructed in substantial conformity with the plans and specifications on file with the City or County and the Seller's lender. I/We acknowledge that the premises were not built to our specifications and that the seller had the right to make such changes as Seller deemed necessary before, during and after the completion of construction and that such changes, if any, have been accepted by the County or City and Seller's lender, and that we are purchasing the completed residential property above mentioned. During my/our inspection, all other improvements, fixtures, equipment, decoration, suitability and readiness of use as my/our home which I/We are purchasing are complete and acceptable, with the exceptions listed hereon:

KITCHEN AREA:
Range Top *left rear burner knob missing*
Range Hood *ok*
Oven *broiler pan missing*
Dishwasher *front panel dented*
Disposal *rubber splash guard missing*
Kitchen Sink *chip right tap edge*
All tile *crack - left of sink*
Cabinets *door knob missing over range hood*
Light Fixtures *ok*
Floors *vinyl gouged, front of dishwasher*

BATH #2:
Glass Enclosure *ok*
Ceramic Tile *ok*
Cultured Marble (Tops) *scratch right of sink*
Stool *lid scratched*
Lavatory *ok*
Light Fixtures *plastic panel cracked*
Floors *need caulking at tub*

BATH #1:
Glass Enclosure *doors hard to slide*
Tub *stopper missing*
Ceramic Tile *bad fit at light switch*
Cultured Marble (Tops) *ok*
Stool *ok*
Lavatory *left door under sink warped*
Light Fixtures *ok*
Floors *base shoe missing behind door*

HALF BATH:
Stool Lavatory *seat + TP roller missing*
Cultured Marble (Tops) *cigarette burn left side*
Light Fixtures *globe missing*
Floors *ok*

LINING ROOM:
Walls *ok - Ceiling gouged at kitchen entry*
Light Fixtures *not as ordered*

LIVING ROOM:
Walls *bad texture under window*
seam in carpet not tight

BEDROOMS:

	1	2	3	4	5
Wardrobe	ok	not painted inside	pole missing	ok	
Walls	ok	dent behind door	ok	gap left of window	
Light Fixtures	outlet cover missing	ok	ok	ok	
Floors	bad squeak - center	ok	ok	vinyl tile cracked at closet	
Miscellaneous	screen missing	door knob dented	ok	door doesn't latch	

EXTERIOR:
rear of front facia board unpainted; front hose bib handle missing; front left corner of driveway cracked; splash block missing under rear down spout; side garage door won't lock; patch stucco left of garage door.

ADDITIONAL ITEMS:
hot water heater vent pipe not painted; glass cracked in fixture at side garage door; fireplace damper hard to operate.

Homeowner acknowledges and accepts the findings of the mutual inspections.

DATE: *June 21, 1986*

BY: *S. Jones*
COMPANY REPRESENTATIVE

DATE: *6/21/86*

BY: *John Doe*
Jane Doe
BUYERS

THE NEW HOUSE BUYER'S GUIDE $18.95, postpaid

Name _____

Address _____

City _____ State ____ Zip ____

Charge my ☐ VISA ☐ MasterCard

Account # _____

Interbank number for MasterCard _____

(please print)
Exp. date _____

Cardholder's Name _____

Cardholder signature _____

CA residents $20.09 which includes 6% tax.

Allow three weeks for delivery

FILL OUT THIS POSTAGE FREE CARD AND MAIL TODAY

SEND THIS THOUGHTFUL GIFT TO MY FRIEND/NEIGHBOR:

Name _____

Address _____

City _____ State ____ Zip ____

Charge my ☐ VISA ☐ MasterCard

Account # _____

Interbank number for MasterCard _____

(please print)
Exp. date _____

Cardholder's Name _____

Cardholder signature _____

CA residents $20.09 which includes 6% tax.

Allow three weeks for delivery

FILL OUT THIS POSTAGE FREE CARD AND MAIL TODAY

THE NEW HOUSE BUYER'S GUIDE $18.95, postpaid

Please send copy to:

Name _____

Address _____

City _____ State ____ Zip ____

Charge my ☐ VISA ☐ MasterCard

Account # _____

Interbank number for MasterCard _____

(please print)
Exp. date _____

Cardholder's Name _____

Cardholder signature _____

CA residents $20.09 which includes 6% tax.

Allow three weeks for delivery

FILL OUT THIS POSTAGE FREE CARD AND MAIL TODAY

COMMUNICATE WITH THE AUTHOR

How did you hear about this book? _____

Did you ☐ Buy it?   ☐ Receive it as a gift?

What information was most helpful? _____

_____

_____

Price range of your new house $_____

Would you be interested in a follow-up newsletter

☐ Yes   ☐ No

Topics you'd like covered: _____

_____

_____

_____

_____

_____

Comments: _____

_____

_____

Name: _____

Address: _____

City _____ State ____ Zip ____

FILL OUT THIS POSTAGE FREE CARD AND MAIL TODAY

**NO POSTAGE
NECESSARY
IF MAILED
IN THE
UNITED STATES**

BUSINESS REPLY MAIL
FIRST CLASS MAIL PERMIT NO. 243 THOUSAND OAKS, CA

POSTAGE WILL BE PAID BY ADDRESSEE

CAREFREE LIVING CO.
2509 E. THOUSAND OAKS BLVD #160
THOUSAND OAKS, CA 91362-9957

**NO POSTAGE
NECESSARY
IF MAILED
IN THE
UNITED STATES**

BUSINESS REPLY MAIL
FIRST CLASS MAIL PERMIT NO. 243 THOUSAND OAKS, CA

POSTAGE WILL BE PAID BY ADDRESSEE

CAREFREE LIVING CO.
2509 E. THOUSAND OAKS BLVD #160
THOUSAND OAKS, CA 91362-9957

**NO POSTAGE
NECESSARY
IF MAILED
IN THE
UNITED STATES**

BUSINESS REPLY MAIL
FIRST CLASS MAIL PERMIT NO. 243 THOUSAND OAKS, CA

POSTAGE WILL BE PAID BY ADDRESSEE

CAREFREE LIVING CO.
2509 E. THOUSAND OAKS BLVD #160
THOUSAND OAKS, CA 91362-9957

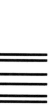

**NO POSTAGE
NECESSARY
IF MAILED
IN THE
UNITED STATES**

BUSINESS REPLY MAIL
FIRST CLASS MAIL PERMIT NO. 243 THOUSAND OAKS, CA

POSTAGE WILL BE PAID BY ADDRESSEE

CAREFREE LIVING CO.
2509 E. THOUSAND OAKS BLVD #160
THOUSAND OAKS, CA 91362-9957

THE NEW HOUSE BUYER'S GUIDE $18.95, postpaid

SEND THIS THOUGHTFUL GIFT TO MY FRIEND/NEIGHBOR:

Name _____

Address _____

City _____ State _____ Zip _____

Charge my ☐ VISA ☐ MasterCard

Cardholder's Name _____

Account # _____ (please print) Exp. date _____

Interbank number for MasterCard _____

Cardholder signature _____

CA residents $20.09 which includes 6% tax.

Allow three weeks for delivery

THE NEW HOUSE BUYER'S GUIDE $18.95, postpaid

SEND THIS THOUGHTFUL GIFT TO MY FRIEND/NEIGHBOR:

Name _____

Address _____

City _____ State _____ Zip _____

Charge my ☐ VISA ☐ MasterCard

Cardholder's Name _____

Account # _____ (please print) Exp. date _____

Interbank number for MasterCard _____

Cardholder signature _____

CA residents $20.09 which includes 6% tax.

Allow three weeks for delivery

THE NEW HOUSE BUYER'S GUIDE $18.95, postpaid

Please send copy to:

Name _____

Address _____

City _____ State _____ Zip _____

Charge my ☐ VISA ☐ MasterCard

Cardholder's Name _____

Account # _____ (please print) Exp. date _____

Interbank number for MasterCard _____

Cardholder signature _____

CA residents $20.09 which includes 6% tax.

Allow three weeks for delivery

COMMUNICATE WITH THE AUTHOR

How did you hear about this book? _____

Did you ☐ Buy it? ☐ Receive it as a gift?

What information was most helpful? _____

_____

_____

Price range of your new house $_____

Would you be interested in a follow-up newsletter

☐ Yes ☐ No

Topics you'd like covered: _____

_____

_____

_____

_____

_____

_____

Comments: _____

_____

_____

Name: _____

Address: _____

City _____ State _____ Zip _____

NO POSTAGE
NECESSARY
IF MAILED
IN THE
UNITED STATES

BUSINESS REPLY MAIL

FIRST CLASS MAIL PERMIT NO. 243 THOUSAND OAKS, CA

POSTAGE WILL BE PAID BY ADDRESSEE

CAREFREE LIVING CO.
2509 E. THOUSAND OAKS BLVD #160
THOUSAND OAKS, CA 91362-9957

NO POSTAGE
NECESSARY
IF MAILED
IN THE
UNITED STATES

BUSINESS REPLY MAIL

FIRST CLASS MAIL PERMIT NO. 243 THOUSAND OAKS, CA

POSTAGE WILL BE PAID BY ADDRESSEE

CAREFREE LIVING CO.
2509 E. THOUSAND OAKS BLVD #160
THOUSAND OAKS, CA 91362-9957

NO POSTAGE
NECESSARY
IF MAILED
IN THE
UNITED STATES

BUSINESS REPLY MAIL

FIRST CLASS MAIL PERMIT NO. 243 THOUSAND OAKS, CA

POSTAGE WILL BE PAID BY ADDRESSEE

CAREFREE LIVING CO.
2509 E. THOUSAND OAKS BLVD #160
THOUSAND OAKS, CA 91362-9957

NO POSTAGE
NECESSARY
IF MAILED
IN THE
UNITED STATES

BUSINESS REPLY MAIL

FIRST CLASS MAIL PERMIT NO. 243 THOUSAND OAKS, CA

POSTAGE WILL BE PAID BY ADDRESSEE

CAREFREE LIVING CO.
2509 E. THOUSAND OAKS BLVD #160
THOUSAND OAKS, CA 91362-9957

KITCHEN

RANGE TOP _____
(look for scratches, dents, missing parts)

RANGE HOOD _____
(look for scratches, dents, missing parts, overall operation)

OVEN(S) STANDARD _____
(look for scratches, dents, missing parts)

OVEN-MICROWAVE _____
(check for scratches, dents, missing parts)

DISHWASHER _____
(check for scratches, dents, missing parts)

TRASH COMPACTOR _____
(check for scratches, dents, is it fastened securely to cabinet?)

DISPOSAL _____
(check operation)

KITCHEN SINK _____
(check for scratches, chips)

COUNTER TOPS _____
(check for scratches, chips, gouges, cracks)

CABINETS _____
(check for scratches, warped doors, open all drawers & doors)

LIGHT FIXTURES _____
(check for operationn, cracked or missing parts)

FLOORS _____
(check for scratches, gouges, eveness, color match)

WALLS & CEILING _____
(check for dents, gouges, nail pops, bad joints)

WINDOWS _____
(check ease of operation, locks, scratched glass, screen)

DOORS _____
(check ease of opening & closing, do they latch properly?)

OTHER _____

_____

_____

LIVING ROOM

CEILING _____
(check for even texture, cracks, holes, even color)

WALLS _____
(check for nail pops, eveness of texture, holes or cracks)

FLOOR _____
(check carpet for eveness of installation and seams)

WINDOWS _____
(check ease of opening, lock mechanism, scratched glass, screen)

FIREPLACE _____
(check damper for ease of operation. check for spark arrestor)

DINING ROOM

CEILING _____
(check for even texture, cracks, holes, even color)

WALLS _____
(check for nail pops, eveness of texture, holes or cracks or gouges)

FLOOR _____
(check carpet for eveness of installation and seams)

WINDOWS _____
(check ease of opening, lock mechanism, scratched glass, screen)

OTHER _____

FAMILY ROOM

CEILING _____
(check for even texture, cracks, holes, even color)

WALLS _____
(check for nail pops, eveness of texture, holes or cracks or gouges)
If panelled, check for eveness of walls and general overall appearance)

FLOOR _____
(if carpet, check as above. If wood or vinyl, check for scratches
eveness and overall appearance)

WINDOWS _____
(check ease of opening, lock mechanism, scratched glass, screen)

FIREPLACE _____
(check damper for ease of operation. check for spark arrestor)

MASTER BATHROOM

GLASS ENCLOSURE
TUB & SHOWER _____
       (do doors open & close smoothly? check for neat installation)

TUB _____
       (check for scratches & chips, check stopper)

CERAMIC TILE_____
       (look for cracked or broken tiles, loose grout joints)

COUNTER TOPS _____
       (should be scratch free and not cracked or chipped)

VANITY CABINETS_____
       (check doors and drawers)

MEDICINE CABINETS _____
       (inspect mirror, see that shelves are installed)

TOILET _____
       (flush, check leaks around base, seat lid for scratches)

SINK _____
       (look for scratches or chips, check stopper)

LIGHT FIXTURES _____
       (check for missing or broken parts)

WALLS & CEILING _____
       (check for nail pops, cracks, unevenness of paint & texture)

FLOORS_____
       (if carpet, check neatness of installation. If vinyl, look
       for scratches, gouges or unevenness. Is base shoe installed?)

WINDOWS_____
       (check ease of opening, lock, scratched glass, screen)

OTHER _____

_____

_____

_____

BATHROOM #2

GLASS ENCLOSURE
TUB & SHOWER _____
      (do doors open & close smoothly? check for neat installation)

TUB _____
      (check for scratches & chips, check stopper)

CERAMIC TILE_____
      (look for cracked or broken tiles, loose grout joints)

COUNTER TOPS _____
      (should be scratch free and not cracked or chipped)

VANITY CABINETS_____
      (check doors and drawers)

MEDICINE CABINETS _____
      (inspect mirror, see that shelves are installed)

TOILET _____
      (flush, check leaks around base, seat lid for scratches)

SINK _____
      (look for scratches or chips, check stopper)

LIGHT FIXTURES _____
      (check for missing or broken parts)

WALLS & CEILING _____
      (check for nail pops, cracks, uneveness of paint & texture)

FLOORS_____
      (if carpet, check neatness of installation. If vinyl, look
      for scratches, gouges or uneveness. Is base shoe installed?)

WINDOWS_____
      (check ease of opening, lock, scratched glass, screen)

OTHER _____

_____

_____

_____

BATHROOM #3

GLASS ENCLOSURE
TUB & SHOWER _____
(do doors open & close smoothly? check for neat installation)

TUB _____
(check for scratches & chips, check stopper)

CERAMIC TILE _____
(look for cracked or broken tiles, loose grout joints)

COUNTER TOPS _____
(should be scratch free and not cracked or chipped)

VANITY CABINETS _____
(check doors and drawers)

MEDICINE CABINETS _____
(inspect mirror, see that shelves are installed)

TOILET _____
(flush, check leaks around base, seat lid for scratches)

SINK _____
(look for scratches or chips, check stopper)

LIGHT FIXTURES _____
(check for missing or broken parts)

WALLS & CEILING _____
(check for nail pops, cracks, uneveness of paint & texture)

FLOORS _____
(if carpet, check neatness of installation. If vinyl, look
for scratches, gouges or uneveness. Is base shoe installed?)

WINDOWS _____
(check ease of opening, lock, scratched glass, screen)

OTHER _____

_____

_____

_____

BATHROOM #4

GLASS ENCLOSURE
TUB & SHOWER _____
       (do doors open & close smoothly? check for neat installation)

TUB _____
       (check for scratches & chips, check stopper)

CERAMIC TILE_____
       (look for cracked or broken tiles, loose grout joints)

COUNTER TOPS _____
       (should be scratch free and not cracked or chipped)

VANITY CABINETS_____
       (check doors and drawers)

MEDICINE CABINETS _____
       (inspect mirror, see that shelves are installed)

TOILET _____
       (flush, check leaks around base, seat lid for scratches)

SINK _____
       (look for scratches or chips, check stopper)

LIGHT FIXTURES _____
       (check for missing or broken parts)

WALLS & CEILING _____
       (check for nail pops, cracks, uneveness of paint & texture)

FLOORS_____
       (if carpet, check neatness of installation. If vinyl, look
       for scratches, gouges or uneveness. Is base shoe installed?)

WINDOWS_____
       (check ease of opening, lock, scratched glass, screen)

OTHER _____

_____

_____

_____

POWDER ROOM

CERAMIC TILE _____
(look for cracked or broken tiles, loose grout joints)

COUNTER TOPS _____
(should be scratch free and not cracked or chipped)

VANITY CABINETS _____
(check doors and drawers)

MEDICINE CABINETS _____
(inspect mirror, see that shelves are installed)

TOILET _____
(flush, check leaks around base, seat lid for scratches)

SINK _____
(look for scratches or chips, check stopper)

LIGHT FIXTURES _____
(check for missing or broken parts)

WALLS & CEILING _____
(check for nail pops, cracks, uneveness of paint & texture)

FLOORS _____
(if carpet, check neatness of installation. If vinyl, look
for scratches, gouges or uneveness. Is base shoe installed?)

WINDOWS _____
(check ease of opening, lock, scratched glass, screen)

OTHER _____

_____

_____

_____

_____

_____

BEDROOM #1

CEILINGS _____
(check for texture eveness, cracks or holes)

WALLS _____
(check for nail pops, texture eveness, holes or cracks)

WARDROBE DOORS _____
(check ease of operation, scratches or dents)

MAIN DOOR _____
(check latch mechanism, check ease of operation)

FLOOR COVERING _____
(check carpet for eveness. If vinyl, check for scratches & seams)

WINDOWS_____
(check ease of opening, lock mechanism, scratched glass, screen)

CLOSETS _____
(check ceiling, walls, clothes poles & shelves)

OTHER _____

_____

BEDROOM #2

CEILINGS _____
(check for texture eveness, cracks or holes)

WALLS _____
(check for nail pops, texture eveness, holes or cracks)

WARDROBE DOORS _____
(check ease of operation, scratches or dents)

MAIN DOOR _____
(check latch mechanism, check ease of operation)

FLOOR COVERING _____
(check carpet for eveness. If vinyl, check for scratches & seams)

WINDOWS_____
(check ease of opening, lock mechanism, scratched glass, screen)

CLOSETS _____
(check ceiling, walls, clothes poles & shelves)

OTHER _____

_____

BEDROOM #3

CEILINGS _____
(check for texture eveness, cracks or holes)

WALLS _____
(check for nail pops, texture eveness, holes or cracks)

WARDROBE DOORS _____
(check ease of operation, scratches or dents)

MAIN DOOR _____
(check latch mechanism, check ease of operation)

FLOOR COVERING _____
(check carpet for eveness. If vinyl, check for scratches & seams)

WINDOWS_____
(check ease of opening, lock mechanism, scratched glass, screen)

CLOSETS _____
(check ceiling, walls, clothes poles & shelves)

OTHER _____

_____

BEDROOM #4

CEILINGS _____
(check for texture eveness, cracks or holes)

WALLS _____
(check for nail pops, texture eveness, holes or cracks)

WARDROBE DOORS _____
(check ease of operation, scratches or dents)

MAIN DOOR _____
(check latch mechanism, check ease of operation)

FLOOR COVERING _____
(check carpet for eveness. If vinyl, check for scratches & seams)

WINDOWS_____
(check ease of opening, lock mechanism, scratched glass, screen)

CLOSETS _____
(check ceiling, walls, clothes poles & shelves)

OTHER _____

_____

LAUNDRY ROOM

CEILINGS & WALLS _____
          (check for nail pops, smoothness of paint coverage, holidays)

DOORS _____
                    (check door locks and latches)

WINDOW _____
                  (check ease of opening, lock and screen)

LIGHT FIXTURE _____
                  (check for missing, broken or cracked parts)

FLOOR _____
            (check vinyl for gouges, tears. Check tile for cracks, grout)

DRYER CONNECTION _____ VENT _____
                        (gas or electric)   (is it installed?)

OTHER _____
              (are water faucets and drain outlet for washer installed?)

_____

_____

_____

_____

_____

GARAGE

WALLS & CEILING _____
(check finished areas for cracks & holes)

MAIN DOOR(S)_____
(check ease of operation, proper fit, locking mechanism,
automatic opener, if any)

OTHER DOORS _____
(check side or rear doors for operation, check locks)

FLOOR _____
(check for cracks in slab, proper slope toward front)

ELECTRICAL _____
(check for outlets, ceiling lights and opener outlet)

OTHER _____

_____

ATTIC

ATTIC ACCESS _____
(determine location. if ceiling hole, check for proper fit)

INSULATION _____
(how thick? is hatch cover insulated? get certificate)

VENTILATION _____
(check for proper ventilation. see that holes are screened)

STAIRWAY _____
(check for sturdiness, handrail, ease of operation if pull-down)

OTHER _____

_____

BASEMENT

STAIRWAY _____
(check for sturdiness, handrail for safety)

WALLS _____
(look for cracks and evidence of water leakage)

FLOOR _____
(look for cracks and any water stains)

OTHER _____

_____

EXTERIOR

DRIVEWAY, PAVED PATHWAYS,
SIDEWALKS _____
(check for cracks, broken corners, deep depressions or raised
portions)

FENCES _____
(check for sturdiness. Has all fencing been installed per contract?)

HOUSE EXTERIOR _____
(check siding material for color match, texture continuity,
symmetry. if stucco or masonry, any cracks wider than 1/8 inch
should be repaired)

_____

_____

ROOF _____
(check for continuity and symmetry of roofing materials. check
for any broken or missing pieces)

_____

GUTTERS AND
DOWNSPOUTS _____
(have these items been installed as per contract? Check to see
that roof water from downspouts is either deflected or piped away
from foundation of house)

ELECTRICAL
FIXTURES _____
(see that all of the fixtures have been installed and check for
missing pieces. See that all exterior outlets have waterproof
covers)

LANDSCAPING _____
(make sure that everything per contract has been planted or
installed)

_____

Miscellaneous _____
(have the house numbers been installed? If on a rural route,
has your mailbox been installed? have the outside hose bibs been
installed? etc, etc, etc.)

_____

_____

_____

FINAL CHECK LIST

TAKE WITH YOU:
- ☐ **A measuring tape**
- ☐ **Extra pad of paper to note furniture placement; telephone jacks, wall outlets, etc., before movers arrive.**

ASK LOCATION OF:
- ☐ Electric panel
- ☐ Gas meter
- ☐ Water meter
- ☐ Main water shut-off valve

OBTAIN OWNER'S MANUALS and/or OPERATION INSTRUCTIONS FOR:
- ☐ All appliances; Water heater; Furnace; Air conditioning unit.

- ☐ A list of the service companies who will perform warranty service on these appliances.

  If not already in place:
- ☐ sink strainer baskets
- ☐ garbage disposal splash guard
- ☐ sink faucet aerators
- ☐ bread boards
- ☐ toilet paper holder rollers
- ☐ shower heads
- ☐ fireplace log lighter keys
- ☐ garage door opener remote control units

- ☐ Copy of your builder's walk-through sheet.
- ☐ Insulation certificate.

  Utility company telephone numbers:

gas	_____ - _____
electric	_____ - _____
telephone	_____ - _____
cable tv	_____ - _____
water	_____ - _____

TEST:
- ☐ Wall switches and outlets
- ☐ Garage door opener
- ☐ Flush all toilets

BE SURE:
- ☐ Light bulbs have been installed
- ☐ To make arrangements for gas, elecrtric and telephone to be turned on before you move in.

COMPARE:
- ☐ Builder's walk-through sheet with yours.